Residential Construction

Systems ◆ Materials ◆ Codes

Jerry Germer

NKBA
The Finest Professionals in the Kitchen & Bath Industry
National Kitchen & Bath Association℠

Professional Resource Library

About The National Kitchen & Bath Association

As the only non-profit trade association dedicated exclusively to the kitchen and bath industry, the National Kitchen & Bath Association (NKBA) is the leading source of information and education for all professionals in the field.

NKBA's mission is to enhance member success and excellence by promoting professionalism and ethical business practices, and by providing leadership and direction for the kitchen and bath industry.

A non-profit trade association with more than 25,000 members in North America and overseas, it has provided valuable resources for industry professionals for more than forty years. Its members are the finest professionals in the kitchen and bath industry.

NKBA has pioneered innovative industry research, developed effective business management tools, and set groundbreaking standards for safe, functional and comfortable design of kitchens and baths.

NKBA provides a unique, one-stop resource for professional reference materials, seminars and workshops, distance learning opportunities, marketing assistance, design competitions, consumer referrals, job and internship opportunities and opportunities for volunteer leadership activities.

Recognized as the kitchen and bath industry's education and information leader, NKBA provides development opportunities and continuing education for all levels of professionals. More than 100 courses, as well as a certification program with three internationally recognized levels, help kitchen and bath professionals raise the bar for excellence.

For students entering the industry, NKBA offers Supported and Endorsed Programs, which provide NKBA-approved curriculum at more than 47 learning institutions throughout North America.

NKBA helps members and other industry professionals stay on the cutting-edge of an ever-changing field through the Association's Kitchen/Bath Industry Show, one of the largest trade shows in the country.

NKBA offers membership in four different categories: Industry, Associate, Student and Honorary. Industry memberships are broken into eleven different industry segments. For more information, visit NKBA at www.nkba.org.

THANK YOU TO OUR SPONSORS

The National Kitchen & Bath Association recognizes with gratitude the following companies who generously helped to fund the creation of this industry resource.

PATRONS

www.americanwoodmark.com

www.kohler.com

BENEFACTORS

www.ge.com

www.subzero.com

www.wolfappliance.com

CONTRIBUTOR

www.groheamerica.com

SUPPORTERS

www.nyloft.net

www.showhouse.moen.com

TOTO®

www.totousa.com

DONORS

Rev-A-Shelf | **Viking Range** | **Whirlpool**

This book is intended for professional use by residential kitchen and bath designers. The procedures and advice herein have been shown to be appropriate for the applications described; however, no warranty (expressed or implied) is intended or given. Moreover, the user of this book is cautioned to be familiar with and to adhere to all manufacturers' planning, installation and use/care instructions. In addition, the user is urged to become familiar with and adhere to all applicable local, state and federal building codes, licensing and legislation requirements governing the user's ability to perform all tasks associated with design and installation standards, and to collaborate with licensed practitioners who offer professional services in the technical areas of mechanical, electrical and load bearing design as required for regulatory approval, as well as health and safety regulations.

Information about this book and other association programs
and publications may be obtained from the
National Kitchen & Bath Association
687 Willow Grove Street, Hackettstown, New Jersey 07840
Phone (800) 843-6522
www.nkba.org

ISBN 1-887127-51-8

First Edition 2006

Illustrations by: Jerry Germer

Top cover photo courtesy Larry A. Falke Photography – Lake Forest, CA
Bottom cover photo courtesy Sandra L. Steiner-Houck, CKD – Mechanicsburg, PA

Published on behalf of NKBA by Fry Communications, Irvine, CA

Peer Reviewers

Timothy Aden, CMKBD	Jim Krengel, CMKBD
Julia Beamish, Ph.D, CKE	Chris LaSpada, CPA
Leonard V. Casey	Elaine Lockard
Ellen Cheever, CMKBD, ASID	Phyllis Markussen, Ed.D, CKE, CBE
Hank Darlington	Chris J Murphy, CKD, CBD, CKBI
Dee David, CKD, CBD	David Newton, CMKBD
Peggy Deras, CKD, CID	Roberta Null, Ph.D
Kimball Derrick, CKD	Michael J Palkowitsch, CMKBD
Tim DiGuardi	Paul Pankow, CKBI
Kathleen Donohue, CMKBD	Jack Parks
Gretchen L. Edwards, CMKBD	Kathleen R. Parrott, Ph.D, CKE
JoAnn Emmel, Ph.D	Al Pattison,CMKBD
Jerry Germer	Les Petrie, CMKBD
Pietro A. Giorgi, Sr., CMKBD	Becky Sue Rajala, CKD
Tom Giorgi	Betty L. Ravnik, CKD, CBD
Jerome Hankins, CKD	Robert Schaefer
Spencer Hinkle, CKD	Klaudia Spivey, CMKBD
Max Isley, CMKBD	Kelly Stewart, CMKBD
Mark Karas, CMKBD	Tom Trzcinski, CMKBD
Martha Kerr, CMKBD	Stephanie Witt, CMKBD

PART ONE: THE BIG PICTURE

CHAPTER 1: The House and Its Parts

To succeed in the exciting but demanding field of kitchen and bath design you need expertise in two important areas: interpersonal communications and technical knowledge.

Strong communication skills enable you to understand your clients' needs so you can then conceive design solutions that will satisfy them. And those same skills allow you to effectively communicate with the many other professionals on the project—architects, general contractors and various subcontractors and installers—who translate your design from a two-dimensional plan into a three-dimensional reality.

Because your design must not only meet the client's expectations but also be feasible to build, you'll also need a solid understanding of the technical aspects of building construction. Kitchens and baths are parts of a whole house—so understanding the structure and components of a house is essential for this kind of work. And dealing with the unexpected will pose a constant challenge, particularly in remodeling work. Can you tear out that wall without jeopardizing the floor or roof above? What lurks beneath that plaster with the suspicious wet spots on the surface? How can you ensure that the floor in the bath will support the weight of a new spa? These are the types of technical questions this book addresses.

This book will introduce you to the basics of residential construction and how to deal with some typical issues that may arise in your work as a designer. Specific aims of this book are to help you understand:

- The various parameters that affect your design.

- Typical building systems used in home construction.

- The elements that make up the foundation, floors, walls and roof of a home.

- Emerging systems and quality techniques that will enhance your design.

- Problems in existing construction that can affect your design.

Understanding how a house is constructed is much simpler if you study one part at a time. So this book breaks the house down into **systems**. A system is **an assembly of parts that work together toward a common goal**.

The goal of a house is to shelter the inhabitants, and the several systems that make up the whole each contribute to this goal in some way. Because the human body comprises a number of systems that parallel those of a house, we'll use it as an example.

A QUICK TOUR OF THE SYSTEMS IN A HOUSE

Our quick tour of the major systems of a house begins with its **structural system—the foundation, walls, floors** and **roof**—that form the skeleton of the building, and the concrete, studs, beams, columns and fasteners that constitute the bones of the structural system.

The most basic part, the foundation, anchors the rest of the structural system, or superstructure, to the earth. Walls, in turn, rise above the foundation to support the floors and roof. To do this, walls must resist both the lateral forces of winds and earth movement and the vertical forces of the structure and its contents. The weight of snow is an added burden for the roofs of most houses in North America. When you hear building professionals talk about *structural changes*, they are referring to changes to the *bones*, as opposed to *cosmetic* alterations that can be made without affecting the structure. Such changes must be made with care to maintain the stability and continuity of the entire system.

The system most akin to the skin in a human body is the **envelope** of the house. Its purpose is to control access to the interior. Climate control is the first charge. A well-designed envelope contains sufficient insulation to control heat loss and gain to the interior and the proper siding and roofing—*skin*—to shelter the interior from wind and water. The envelope system's second task is to provide security and privacy for the occupants, which requires it to be designed to control access and views. Doors and windows in the envelope are the primary means of controlling access. They are also a means of controlling admittance of light and fresh air to the interior.

It takes a myriad of other items inside the envelope to make the structure into a house. The **plumbing system** comprises the water heater, fixtures, water-, waste-, and vent-piping required for water supply to the kitchen and bath areas. Furnaces, heaters and fans constitute the equipment of the **mechanical system** that heats, cools, and ventilates the interior. Networks of ducts, wiring and piping distribute the heating or cooling to various parts of the house. The **electrical systems** comprise the home's power distribution, lighting, home security, automation, audio-visual equipment, along with the increasingly complicated wiring and control networks required to make these systems operate smoothly.

Finally, a house contains non-structural **interior partitions, cabinets,** and **furnishings**, we don't normally think of as systems, but we can, since they fit the definition of a system as an assembly of parts that work together toward a common goal.

LEARN TO READ THE HOUSE

If your design work involves existing houses—as it most likely will—you'll soon become familiar with the systems. You'll need to develop an ability to sleuth out these in-place systems to be able to plan the alterations in a way that will avoid unpleasant surprises for yourself and the owner.

Start with a jobsite inspection. Standing outside the house, look up to the roof. Note where the plumbing vents emerge. Are they to the left or right of that window you want to enlarge? Is it necessary to move them? You might also look for peeling paint, which can be a sign of poor moisture control from the interior.

When you enter the interior start at the basement or crawl space. You can get a lot of information about the systems of a house down there. The locations of columns or bearing walls, for example, can give you an idea of where the bearing walls are upstairs. The main service panel can tell you if it's possible to add a new double oven without upsizing the panel. The sewer waste line tells you where the main waste/vent stack makes its vertical run up to the roof. Note the locations of ducts and where they make their bends to supply floors above. You'll also get a general idea of the plumbing system, whether it's up-to-date or needs upgrading.

Upstairs, as you walk through the interior pay close attention to the location of heating registers or baseboard strip diffusers. Moving these will also entail changes to the ducts or piping concealed in the floors or walls. Walls and floors abutting plumbing fixtures also contain piping that must be accommodated when fixtures are relocated. With a screwdriver, remove the cover plate from an electrical outlet or switch on an outside wall. You should be able to tell the amount and type of insulation in the wall. Any signs of mold, mildew or dampness on interior surfaces indicate a moisture problem that must be dealt with. Moisture behind fixtures generally traces to leaky fixtures or condensation, both of which can be corrected with good design.

If you can get into the attic, you will be able to tell more about the structural system, including the location of bearing walls, as well as insulation and moisture barriers.

Learning to read a house takes knowledge and experience. You'll get the experience over time in the course of your work. This book will introduce you to the building systems—structural, envelope, and interior that comprise a home's architecture. The plumbing, mechanical, and electrical systems are covered in other books published by the National Kitchen & Bath Association (NKBA). The message of all NKBA books is that good kitchen and bath design goes deeper than just planning for new cabinets or fixtures. It's knowing enough about how these improvements integrate with *all* the parts of the house to ensure that your design not only works, but works within the client's budget and expectations.

CHAPTER 2: Codes and Permits

Constructing almost anything legally requires a building permit. To obtain one usually requires that the proposed construction satisfy the conditions of one or more codes. The codes that apply depend on the location of the project, size and type. If you limit your work to installing cabinets on walls, you may avoid worrying about codes altogether. But you'll probably need to comply with a building code for any rough carpentry required to support the cabinetry. Any plumbing or electrical work proposed falls under the purview of mechanical and electrical codes. Other codes that may apply set standards for fire safety, energy conservation, and handicap accessibility. You'll save time and hassles by finding out which codes apply to your project before beginning any design work. A large municipality may have several codes in force and a building inspection department to enforce them. On the other hand, if you are planning a project for a small rural location, you may find that it has no code in force at all. But before you begin, check to see if there are state codes in force in the locality.

BUILDING CODES

Designers and installers often complain about codes, but in doing so, lose sight of the reason for them. After all, the goal of building codes is to protect the public's safety and welfare by establishing uniform minimum standards.

Until recently, there were three so-called "model codes" in force in the U.S. that set standards for buildings of all types:

- The BOCA *National Building Code*, published by the Building Officials and Code Administrators International (BOCA). Used primarily in the Northeast and Midwest.

- The Uniform Building Code, published by the International Conference of Building Officials (ICBO), and in use in the Western states.

- The Southern Building Code, published by the Southern Building Code Conference International (SBCCI). In use in the majority of Southern states.

A fourth code, *One and Two Family Dwelling Code*, often called the "CABO code" after its publisher, the Council of American Building Officials (CABO), addresses issues of particular concern to detached houses, and as such, has been acceptable to all three model codes for residential construction.

Local municipalities called these codes model codes because they were contrived to serve as models for further refinement or alteration. Some large cities, such as New York City, have their own code. More commonly though, municipalities adopted the applicable model code as-is or amended it to suit local needs. For example, inordinately high danger from hurricanes, fire, or earthquakes caused areas where these are prevalent to amend the model code with stricter requirements.

As this book is being written, we are going through a transitional period in the U.S., while the heretofore model building codes are being phased out by two new codes written for universal acceptance. The *International Building Code (IBC)*, supercedes the three model building codes, while its companion, the *International Residential Code (IRC)* replaces the One and Two Family Dwelling Code.

The International Building Code

One of the reasons designers and installers haven't liked codes is the confusion resulting from their multiplicity. The time was clearly ripe for the building industry to press for a single unified building code that applied to all parts of the U.S. The first concrete steps toward that goal were taken in 1994, with the establishment of an umbrella organization, the International Code Council (ICC). The goal was to create a code that would not only eventually supersede the regional codes in force in the U.S. but would allow other countries to be part of the system in the future. The first draft of the new international code was published three years later for review. The latest version, *International Building Code 2003* is now being adopted by regional code agencies to replace the former codes.

International Residential Code

Like the codes that were combined to create it, the IBC is more attuned to the issues of commercial, institutional and industrial buildings, than to houses. A companion code, the *International Residential Code (IRC)*, addresses issues specific to home design and construction and referenced throughout the *NKBA Kitchen & Bath Planning Guidelines*.

The new IRC covers one- and two-family detached dwellings and apartment buildings up to three stories. It contains a stand-alone set of standards, with chapters on foundations, framing, plumbing, electrical, mechanical, fuel, gas and energy. The code is claimed to be more complete than the only other predecessor code, the *One and Two Family Dwelling Code*, which focuses on residential construction. The new IRC also contains detailed requirements for emerging techniques, such as steel stud construction, frost-protected shallow foundations and insulated concrete forms (ICFs).

Like the CABO code, the IRC code addresses regional variations of such factors as frost depths, snow loads, and termite threat potential. But the IRC surpasses CABO by including criteria for building in areas prone to floods, high winds and seismic activity.

As in the U.S., Canadian model national building, fire and plumbing codes are prepared under a central agency, then adopted and enforced by the provincial and territorial authorities having jurisdiction. Provinces vary as to which codes are in force, so you should find this out before undertaking any work in a Canadian location.

ENERGY CODES

The energy shortages of the 1970s sparked widespread concern for conserving energy in buildings and spawned new technologies for utilizing renewable energy from solar, wind and geothermal sources in homes. Concurrently, new and better ways were found to make buildings less dependent on *any* outside energy source. To encourage conservation in building construction, the federal, state and local governments developed standards, which found their way into various energy codes. The first uniform energy codes were developed under the name **Model Energy Code (MEC)**.

The Model Energy Code accomplishes conservation goals by allowing designers to comply in one of two approaches. The first is to supply design calculations that ensure that the building as a whole meets the **performance standards** of the code. The second—and more often used—is to simply comply with the minimum **prescriptive standards** of the code. The performance-standard route allows designers more flexibility, if they are willing and capable to do the engineering calculations. For example, a large area of glazing may be used in one part of the building if a higher level of insulation is used to compensate in another area. The second, prescriptive-standards approach simply spells out just how much glazing can be used and what R-value the walls must have.

9

The Model Energy Code has now been succeeded by the **International Energy Conservation Code (IECC)**, which is regularly revised by a large body of code officials and industry representatives. The current version (1995) is the basis accepted by the Department of Energy (DOE) for compliance with the federal Energy Policy Act of 1992, which requires federal mortgage lenders to guarantee that participating new homes comply with at least a similar baseline.

Still, only 34 states had adopted mandatory residential energy codes as of 2001; 20 states had codes certified to meet MEC95 and three had codes in force more stringent than the MEC95. The situation is constantly changing, so find out the status of energy code acceptance in your state by contacting your local building department or state energy office.

Many states and municipalities have since either developed their own energy conservation requirements or have adopted a model code. Forty states currently have energy codes in force.

Canadian energy standards are published in the *Model National Energy Code of Canada for Houses* (MNECH), which allows designers to choose the degree of energy efficiency that is appropriate for specific climates and fuel types. The MNECH applies to residential buildings of three stories or fewer, and additions of more than 10 m². Because of the cold climates of Canadian provinces, the emphasis is on high insulation and air-tightness.

ACCESSIBILITY CODES

The push to make buildings more accessible to people with physical limitations was codified into law by the **Americans with Disabilities Act (ADA)**, which became effective in 1992. Because the law applies to buildings of "public accommodation," rather than private dwellings, it won't likely affect your residential work. Even so, the legislation is evidence of a growing concern for accommodating the needs of people who do not conform to the "average" able adult, which has been the model for design in the past.

People in wheelchairs, a growing percentage of elderly and those with impaired sight, mobility or hearing, all use kitchens and baths. So it wouldn't be unusual for you to work with clients with special needs at some point in your career. If and when you do, don't expect to be able to pick a code book off the shelf that tells you everything you need to know about design and construction for disabled persons.

Because the ADA is a civil rights law, it does not specifically address design standards. Guidelines have, however, been issued in various federal publications such as *Fair Housing Accessibility Guidelines; Design Guidelines for Accessible/Adaptable Dwellings*, published by the U.S. Department of Housing and Urban Development, Office of Fair Housing and Urban Development. Contact the housing agencies in your state to see what standards apply. For further design information on accessibility issues, you may wish to obtain the *Kitchen Planning* and *Bath Planning* **books,** also part of the NKBA's *Professional Resource Library*.

PERMITS AND INSPECTIONS

The type and number of permits required for a particular project depend on the extent of the work planned. Most municipalities require a building permit for any new residential construction and for remodeling if it exceeds a specific value. The general contractor normally obtains this permit upon approval of an application and payment of a fee. The fee is normally a percentage of the construction value of the project. A straightforward interior remodeling project may require no other documentation. For new construction expect to submit a site plan, drawn to scale and showing the house on the property, property lines, site setbacks, utility lines, walks and driveway. You may also need a floor plan and exterior elevations.

Plumbing and electrical work often require separate permits. The municipality may require the work to be installed by a licensed plumber or electrician. For each permit granted by a municipality, there will follow at least one inspection. The building permit will trigger an inspection at the time the rough framing is complete and one after the project is complete. Plumbing and electrical work are usually inspected after rough-in is completed but before any finishes are installed. For example, the inspector will check out the electrical rough-in after the wiring is installed but before it is covered by drywall. Plumbing is installed before floor or wall finishes. If your responsibilities for a project extend beyond design to include oversight during the construction phase you will need to be aware of the required inspections and make sure they occur at a time that will prevent construction delays.

Working with Building Officials

Working with local building departments can go smoothly or become a nightmare. In general, the bigger the municipality, the larger the bureaucracy you face in getting permits and inspections. Another difference is the level of expertise. The inspectors of a city building department may be more knowledgeable about codes and construction than those in small rural districts, who may be part-timers with another primary occupation. In any case, there are some general rules of thumb that can help minimize hassles with the local building authority:

- Visit the local building department to familiarize yourself with the process and obtain information about permits, fees and inspection procedures.

- Get a copy of the local zoning ordinance and check its provisions for each project you propose.

- Find out which codes are in force and get a copy of them. Familiarize yourself with the provisions of the codes that affect your sphere of operation.

- While the project is still in the planning/design stage, take preliminary drawings in to get input and advice. You won't get written approval at that stage, but the officials appreciate being consulted while there is still time for changes and you can use their input to make sure your design complies with local laws or regulations.

- Make sure any plans you submit have the professional stamp required (architect, engineer, surveyor).

- Notify the appropriate inspectors in a timely manner when inspections are due.

- Don't be confrontational with building officials. Listen to their concerns, express your own and seek compromise. Sometimes it pays to let some time lapse and tempers cool before you respond. If you feel you are in over your head, seek outside advice of architects, engineers or attorneys before taking on the building department.

The more you know about codes and permits, the less you will see them as obstacles to the progress of a project, and the more they will become simply another task that you can accomplish in a logical sequence.

CHAPTER 3: Designing Healthy Houses

Children with brain damage from ingesting lead paint chips. People getting respiratory diseases from moldy basements. Cancer cases suspected from drinking water contaminated with MBTE or breathing radon gas. Every day seems to bring a new health scare from something lurking in the home. Why? Two reasons. First, we know more today about environmental health hazards than before. Second, today's homes contain numerous synthetic materials—everything from manufactured lumber to carpets and furniture—whose gasses can't escape to the outside as they did in the past, when houses were draftier and contained fewer manufactured materials.

We'll look at some of these health hazards in this chapter and suggest what you can do as a kitchen and bath designer to minimize them in your projects. Doing so will not only create safer, healthier environments for your clients but also result in better jobsite safety for the installers on the job.

AIRBORNE HAZARDS

Human lungs and nasal passages are pretty well equipped to deal with most kinds of natural dust. Saw-cut or router dust ranges around 33 microns or larger (a micron is one millionth of a meter). Particles of this size are not much risk to the lungs, since they are easily expelled, but a definite irritation to the eyes and nose. Other irritants of this class are fibers of mineral wool or fiberglass insulation. Still larger particles such as ordinary sawdust, at around 10 microns or larger, are usually trapped by mucous in the larger respiratory passages and eventually expelled. Really small particles, such as dust from sanding or grinding materials such as wood, drywall or concrete may be as small as 1.3 microns, small enough to be trapped in the lungs to pose a health hazard. If your project responsibilities encompass jobsite supervision, make sure the areas of operation are sealed off from the house with effective temporary dust barriers and that the workers wear goggles, respirators and protective covering for their skin.

Asbestos

Asbestos is a mineral that is as soft and flexible as cotton or flax, yet it is fireproof. Because of this property, it has seen many uses since the dawn of civilization. The ancient Greeks used asbestos for the wicks of the eternal flames of the vestal virgins, as the funeral dress for the cremation of kings and as napkins. In modern times it found uses in many industrial applications, such as insulation for boilers, steam pipes, turbines, ovens, kilns and other high-temperature equipment.

In a 1906 study, a Frenchman determined that there was an uncommonly high mortality rate among asbestos workers, suspecting this was probably due to the amount of dust that accumulated in the poor working conditions. In 1917 and 1918 several studies in the United States concluded that asbestos workers were dying unnaturally young, and in 1924, the first diagnosis of asbestosis was made. England passed laws in 1931 to increase ventilation and to recognize asbestosis as a work-related disease. It took until 1930 for the first autopsy to establish the existence of asbestos lung disease in North America. The following years saw laws passed to allow asbestosis in Workers' Compensation cases. But these laws often allowed only a very short time period after leaving work in which the employee had to file his claim.

Asbestos dust is now recognized as a major health hazard. Although asbestos products have not been used in construction since approximately 1975, the products already in place present a clear danger to individuals involved in repair work and the demolition of structures containing asbestos products. Asbestos particles, smaller than 10 microns, have been linked to lung cancer and other respiratory maladies.

Asbestos may turn up in remodeling of older houses in any of several locations: pipe and duct insulation, ceiling tiles or—less likely—floor tiles. Left undisturbed, the asbestos poses little risk to the occupants. The danger comes when the particles become airborne, or friable, as they often do in remodeling.

Visit the project before you complete the plans. Federal regulations enforced as part of the Clean Air Act now require that facilities be inspected for asbestos prior to demolition or renovation. Contact the appropriate agency in your state to clarify the enforcement and procedures before engaging in any renovation work. If, after testing, asbestos is found on the site, remediation can take several forms:

- Encapsulation, whereby the asbestos-containing material (ACM) is covered with a sealant to prevent fiber release.

- Encasement, whereby the ACM is covered with a hard-setting sealing material.

- Enclosure, whereby the ACM is placed in an airtight barrier.

- Removal from the site.

The appropriate remedy will be determined according to specific federal guidelines. In residential work, removal is the most likely option. But hire a specialized asbestos abatement subcontractor certified to do this type of work. Remodeling work shouldn't begin before the site has been tested and any remedial work certified as completed.

HARMFUL CHEMICALS IN BUILDING MATERIALS

Arsenic

Moisture is a fact of life in most of the U.S. Except for naturally decay-resistant species such as redwood, cedar or cypress, most woods deteriorate under long-term exposure to moisture. Wood in direct contact with concrete, masonry or soil comes in constant contact with moisture, which facilitates attack by insects and fungus. To withstand this onslaught the wood must be naturally rot-resistant or treated with a chemical. The most common chemical treatment to date has been chromated copper arsenic (CCA). So-called "pressure-treated lumber" typically consists of southern yellow pine that has been immersed under pressure in a bath of CCA solution. You can identify this type of wood by a label attached to the end of each piece and by its slightly greenish tinge.

The arsenic used in the compound has come under increasing attack in recent years as a hazard to health. It can be absorbed through the skin by handling the material, through the air by breathing sawdust or smoke from burning the wood or ingested by drinking water contaminated by CCA-treated wood. A 1994 article in *Environmental Building News* called for a phase-out of CCA-treated wood, noting that it is an increasing burden to landfills and its burning creates a significant toxic hazard. More recently, elevated levels of arsenic have been found in playgrounds in Florida, having leached out from CCA-treated wood playground structures. Individual cases crop up from time to time, such as the U.S. Forest Service employee who got arsenic poisoning while building picnic tables and the Washington state

15

homeowner who became permanently disabled from using pressure-treated lumber still wet from treatment to build a swimming raft at his lakefront property.

To protect installers working with CCA-treated wood, The Environmental Protection Agency recommends the following:

- Always wear gloves and a dust mask when cutting CCA-treated wood.

- Protect eyes by wearing goggles.

- If possible, do any cutting outdoors.

- Wash hands before eating, drinking or smoking.

- Wash work clothes exposed to CCA separately from other clothing.

Guidelines for protecting householders are less precise. ˆIn general:

- Don't leave CCA-treated scraps on the jobsite.

- Make sure any CCA-treated wood is enclosed or inaccessible to the inhabitants.

The most likely alternative chemical contender to CCA currently is ammonia copper quaternary (ACQ), said to be 84 times less hazardous during its life cycle than CCA. If you can find it, be prepared to pay at least 5 percent more. Another is copper azole, said to be comparable to ACQ-treated wood.

A more natural solution, and more elegant in exposed applications such as wood decks, is to use a naturally rot-resistant wood such as cedar, redwood, or cypress, but only the heartwood is rot resistant and the increasing scarcity of redwood and cedar has driven up the costs. For decks, you can also now choose among several composite materials made from plastics and wood fibers—all of which are rot resistant.

Site-Applied Wood Preservatives

Cut ends of treated wood (whatever treatment) and any non-rot-resistant species should be spot treated by brushing or dipping in a preservative solution before installing in a location prone to moisture. A typical example in a kitchen/bath job is the inside edge of a plywood countertop cutout that will support a sink. Another is any pipe cutout in a plywood subfloor. Avoid preservatives that contain lindane, pentachlorophenol (PCB) or tributyl tin oxide (TBTO). Instead, use treatments based on borax, soda, potash, linseed oil or beeswax. The label should state whether the substance is toxic or safe.

Formaldehyde

Let's face it. There's no better substrate for vinyl flooring than plywood, and what would we do without particleboard for cabinetry? Unfortunately, these panels achieve their high strength through a process whereby the wood fibers or chips are forced together under high heat and pressure, using formaldehyde-containing bonding agents. Over time the formaldehyde escapes in gaseous form (outgasses), posing a potential health hazard to the occupants. Because these panels have become so widespread in kitchen and bath work you will have a hard time finding good substitutes. What you can do, if you have jobsite supervision, is minimize the health hazards of outgassing by making sure all such materials are not left exposed, but enclosed behind other construction or sealed with paint or an impermeable surfacing material such as plastic laminate or tile.

Volatile Organic Compounds (VOCs)

The fumes from solvents in oil and lacquer paints and adhesives have long been recognized as a health hazard. Many of the coatings, solvents and adhesives typically used in kitchen and bath work contain compounds derived from refining crude oil. These volatile organic compounds (VOCs) are emitted during drying and/or curing and are known carcinogens. VOC-containing paints for residential applications have been phased out and replaced with water as the solvent. Water-base paints are actually an emulsion of latex compounds and labeled as "latex" or "acrylic," to distinguish them from VOC-solvent paints, which are identified as "oil-based" or "alkyd." As a designer you should be familiar with every coating and adhesive you specify, along with the potential risks they may pose to workers or occupants on the job. If and when you must specify chemicals containing VOCs, take whatever measures are necessary to protect the installers and occupants.

Lead

Lead provided a stable, effective pigment for paints up until the 1970s when its toxic effects were finally recognized and it was banned. By then it had already done untold damage to the health of hapless homeowners and professional builders alike, in the form of hypertension, anemia, kidney failure and memory loss. A report in Massachusetts identified 380 cases of severe lead poisoning in construction workers from 1991 to 1995. Of these, 101 were painters. With lead now banned as an ingredient in paint, the main concern today is existing housing, primarily the potential of children eating lead-paint chips and acquiring brain damage as a consequence.

Lead poisoning from paint is, fortunately, avoidable. Like asbestos, undisturbed lead-based paint poses no hazard. But sanding, scraping or burning off the paint creates clouds of lead dust that can be inhaled or swallowed. This makes for difficult decisions when it comes to renovating. Any paint applied before the 1970s likely contains lead and should be analyzed and removed by a specialized lead abatement contractor before other finishes are applied. If you are charged with jobsite supervision, you can minimize your legal vulnerability by having the homeowner get the paint tested and any abatement work done before you begin your operations.

Lead can leach into drinking water from lead pipes found in homes built before 1950 and from lead-based solder. Traditional solder used to join copper water pipes was made of lead and tin. When the acid in soft water runs through the pipes, it releases some of the lead into the water. Lead-free solder containing silver is now required for pipes containing drinking water. If a kitchen/bath remodeling entails extensive replacement to the water pipes, it may be a good idea to test the solder in the remaining pipes and, if found to contain lead, have them re-soldered. Simple test kits are available from building supply stores.

Other Substances

The list continues to expand of construction materials, once thought to be benign, but subsequently found to be toxic. **Mercury** used to be added to latex paints to control bacteria and mildew. The EPA banned it in the early 1970s. Though the ban was subsequently reversed, the paint companies voluntarily discontinued the additive. **Cadmium**, once a reliable paint pigment, is also no longer used.

A POSITIVE APPROACH TO DESIGN

So far we've talked about what to avoid in your design. Understanding these hazards will enable you to competently deal with them in your design work. One of the first things you might do when beginning a project is to ask your clients what special allergies their household members might have. Take this into account with the materials you specify. Design adequate ventilation to not only remove any airborne pathogens resulting from the construction, but also those resulting from the use of the space after the construction is complete.

But don't stop there. Good design goes beyond minimizing hazards to provide positive benefits to the occupants. The goal of the project should be to make their lives better than they were before. As you acquire knowledge and design skills you'll find ways to make sure your designs transcend the merely safe, or adequate to reach the level of wonderful.

Adequately designed lighting, for example will ensure that the users can see what they are doing. Wonderful lighting will incorporate creative light sources, locations, and controls that enable the occupants to direct the light where they want it and create different moods. It extends to finding ways to use sunlight in the space, through creative use of windows and skylights. Colors, forms, and textures can all be used to design spaces that will be delightful, as well as healthy, areas of the home.

CHAPTER 4: Maximizing Energy Efficiency

Kitchens and baths use more energy than any other rooms in the house. Both require lots of hot water. Rural houses with wells must also pump the water to the point of use. Electrical power is required for ventilation to remove odors, moisture and cooking gasses. Then there are the kitchen appliances that have gotten even more prolific in recent years, all of which depend on gas or electricity to operate. Finally, lighting is likely more extensive, especially in kitchens. As energy sources become increasingly expensive, you will be called on to find efficient ways to achieve your design goals. You can do this by combining three strategies:

1. Design an energy-conserving envelope.

2. Use natural energies where possible, to heat, cool and light the interior.

3. Select energy-efficient equipment.

If you pay attention to each of these in your design, you'll not only save your clients money on operating expenses but also provide them with a pleasant, comfortable interior environment. Let's see how each of these strategies comes into play.

AN ENERGY-CONSERVING BUILDING ENVELOPE

An energy-conserving envelope is a building enclosure in which walls and roof exclude heat in the hot seasons and retain it in the cold seasons. Sounds simple enough, but the hitch comes in the form of location. Because each region has its own particular climatic variables, there is no "one size fits all" rule for designing the envelope for optimum energy efficiency. You must first understand your region's climate, and then learn to design the envelope to optimize its assets and minimize liabilities. Doing so will ensure that your clients will be comfortable year-round, whether they live in Fargo or Houston.

Thermal Insulation

Heat enters and leaves the building primarily by **conduction** through the envelope, though **radiation** and **convection** play a part. The best way to minimize conduction is by insulating the parts of the envelope that have direct contact with the outside weather—the exterior walls and the roof/ceiling. Include the floor in the equation if it sits above a ventilated crawl space.

No matter where the home is geographically located, it needs some amount of thermal insulation in the envelope to control heat gain and loss. If your kitchen/bath project is an addition, don't rely on the existing insulation of the house as a standard for the addition—use the current recommended standards for your calculations and encourage the owner to upgrade the rest of the house if possible.

The standard for rating insulation is its **R-value**, an index of the ability of the material to resist heat flow by conduction. The higher the number, the more conductive heat it blocks. Determine the recommend levels of insulation for your region by contacting your state energy department or local building inspection department. You can get a general idea of the appropriate R-values from the following map and table.

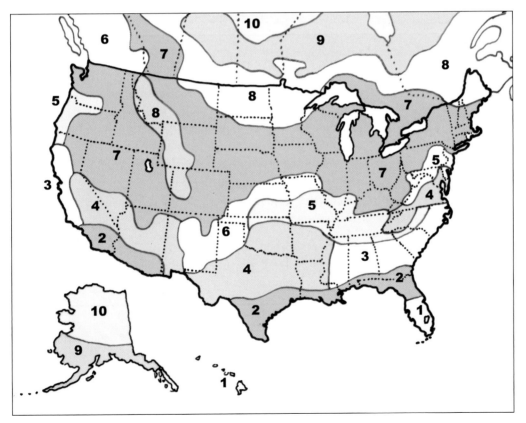

Figure 4.1 Zones for recommended R-values.

RECOMMENDED MINIMUM TOTAL R-VALUES					
Insulation Zone	Ceilings[1]		Floors[2]	Walls	Foundations[3]
	Oil, Gas, Heat Pump	Electric Resistance	All Fuels	All Fuels	All Fuels
1	19	30	0	19	11
2	30	30	0	19	19
3	30	38	0	19	19
4	30	38	19	19	19
5	38	38	19	19	19
6	38	38	19	19	19
7	38	49	19	19	19
8	49	49	19	19	19
9	49	49	19	19	19
10	55	55	19	19	19

[1]Cathedral ceilings and ceilings below ventilated attics
[2]Recommended levels for floors above crawl spaces or basements with uninsulated foundations
[3]Recommended levels for foundation walls if floors are not insulated

Choosing the right type of insulation from the many available options requires matching the insulation to the application, balancing R-values with cost and weighing the ease or difficulty of installation. If your clients will be living in the house during the construction period, you must also consider their convenience. The chart, "Comparing Types of Insulation" on page 26, rates some of the most likely candidates used in homes. Here's a brief description of the major contenders:

Blankets and Batts. Fiberglass and mineral wool blanket and batt insulation is likely the most widely used type of insulation in homes. Thicknesses range between 3 to 12 inches (76 mm to 305 mm), with R-values ranging between R-11 and R-38. Widths are sized to fit between framing members spaced 16 inch (406 mm) or 24 inch (610 mm) centers. Insulation is packed into bundles containing 4-foot-long batts or rolled blankets.

Fiberglass blanket/batt insulation consists of glass fibers pressed together with a binding substance. The standard type is messy to work with. As fibers come loose, they cause the skin to itch and eyes and nose to run. The binder has been improved in some brands to lessen the scratching and keep the fibers from breaking off and becoming airborne. A still newer innovation is a plastic wrap that completely encloses the batt. Fiberglass batts and blankets also come unfaced, for friction fitting between framing and faced with Kraft paper or foil that you staple to the face of the framing. The foil facing can also serve as a vapor barrier, but only if the edges are thoroughly sealed with tape or caulk. Kraft paper facing is only a marginal vapor barrier. Mineral wool, sometimes called rock wool, costs slightly more than fiberglass. It is similar to fiberglass in facings and installation, but an even greater irritation to the skin, eyes and nasal passages.

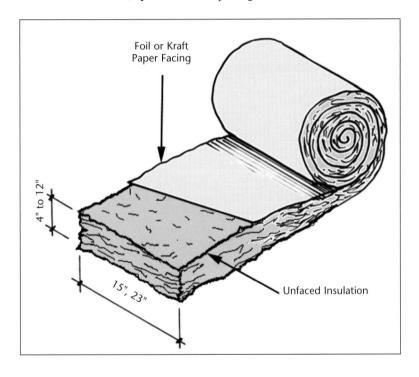

Foil or Kraft
Paper Facing

4" to 12"

15", 23"

Unfaced Insulation

Figure 4.2 Fiberglass or mineral wool batt and blanket insulation is available in various thicknesses and widths sized to fit between framing spaced 16 or 24 inches (406 mm, 610 mm) on center.

Rigid Foam Insulation. Various plastics are foamed into sheet insulation 2 or 4 feet wide, 8 feet long and from 1/2 to 4 inches thick (610 mm or 1,219 mm wide, 2,438 mm long and from 13 mm to 102 mm thick). A higher R-value offsets its higher cost over batt/blanket insulation per inch thickness

The main uses of rigid insulation in homes are on the outside of foundations and undersides of concrete slabs. Rigid foam sheets also provide a way to increase the R-value of an existing stud wall or cathedral ceiling without tearing the wall or ceiling apart. The foil that faces some types can serve as a vapor barrier if the joints are taped. Rigid foam cuts easily with a sharp knife and can be secured by nails, screws or adhesives. Tin washers must be used with nails and screws to keep the heads from punching through the surface.

Figure 4.3 Rigid foam insulation is available faced with foil or unfaced in 2- and 4-foot-wide sheets, 8-feet long (610 mm- and 1,219 mm-wide sheets, 2,438 mm long), in thicknesses up to 6 inches (152 mm). The total R-value depends on the type of foam and thickness.

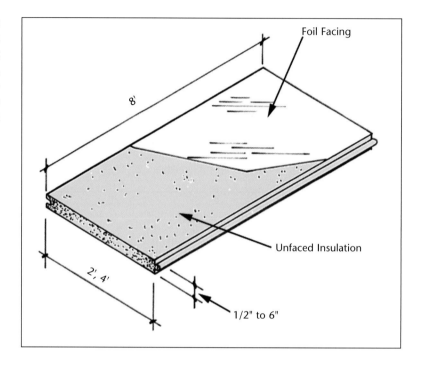

Foamed-in-Place Insulation. Polyurethane and polyisocyanurate, two types of plastic foam used to make rigid sheets, can also be applied in liquid form with special equipment. They offer the highest R-value per inch, excellent resistance to moisture passage and the benefit of completely filling all voids—a real plus for certain floor or wall cavities that can't feasibly be insulated with other products. Franchised applicators apply the liquid foam with nozzles, allowing enough space for the foam to expand. When it cures, it forms a hard film over the surface. Any foam that expands outside the cavities is trimmed off with special tools. Because of its high cost, this method is rarely used in residential applications.

Loose Fill Insulation. Making remodeling work weather-tight often requires insulating nooks and crannies hard to fill with other types. Cellulose, Perlite, fiberglass and mineral wool are available as loose fibers or pellets and bagged for pouring by hand into these hard-to-reach areas or for blowing into walls or ceilings by pneumatic equipment. Cellulose insulation is made from recycled newspapers treated with a fire-retarding chemical. Its R-value is slightly lower than fiberglass or mineral wool, but its slightly greater density makes it less susceptible to being blown about by sudden gusts whipping through the attic. Its main drawback is its tendency to attract and hold moisture, making a good vapor barrier mandatory.

Sprayed Cellulose. The same cellulose available as loose fill can be sprayed into building cavities with pneumatic equipment. It is sprayed dry into horizontal areas such as floors and attics and mixed with water and adhesives and sprayed wet into vertical wall cavities. Damp-sprayed cellulose then clings to the cavities without falling down. After drying, the excess material is scraped (scrubbed) flush with the stud faces. Its ability to completely fill the voids, lack of need for a separate vapor barrier (some claim) and a cost just slightly above fiberglass batts, have made this type of insulation increasingly popular for houses in recent years.

Radiant Barriers. Thermal insulation isn't quite as effective for keeping the sun's heat out of roofs and attics as is another class of materials called radiant barriers. Where thermal insulation blocks conduction only, radiant barriers have a shiny metallic surface that reflects the sun's radiant heat. Radiant barrier materials are available as rigid sheets of foil-faced foam or plywood and rolls of flexible sheet. They are of greatest benefit to homes south of the Mason-Dixon line. To be most effective, radiant barriers must be installed with an airspace between the reflective layer and an adjacent material. The preferred installation in a roof is to place the radiant barrier just below the roof sheathing with the shiny surface facing into the attic.

COMPARING TYPES OF INSULATION

Key: • Usually Sometimes L Low M Medium H High	R per inch	Relative cost	Suitable Applications				
			Vapor barrier integral	Wall/ceiling cavities	Over wall/ceiling surfaces	Foundations	Under concrete slabs
Blanket and Batt Insulation							
Fiberglass, 15" (381 mm), 23" (584 mm) wide, various lengths	3.3	L	[1]	•			
Mineral Wool, 15" (381 mm), 23" (584 mm) wide, various lengths	3.6	L	[1]	•			
Rigid Sheet Insulation							
Phenolic Foam, 4'x8' (1,219 mm x 2,438 mm)	8.5	H	•[2]		•	•	•
Polyurethane, Isocyanurate, 4'x8' (1,219 mm x 2,438 mm) sheets	7.2	M	•[2]		•	•	•
Extruded Polystyrene, 4'x8' (1,219 mm x 2,438 mm), 2'x8' (610 mm x 2,438 mm)	5.0	M			•	•	•
Expanded Polystyrene (beadboard) 4'x8' (1,219 mm x 2,438 mm), 2'x8' (610 mm x 2,438 mm)	4.0	M			•	•	•
Foamed-in-Place Insulation							
Urethane, polyurethane, polyisocyanurate	6.1	H	•[4]	•			
Loose Fill Insulation							
Cellulose, blown in	3.7	M		•			
Cellulose, bagged	3.7	L		•			
Perlite pellets, bagged	2.7	L		•			
Fiberglass, blown in	2.2	M		•			
Mineral Wool, blown in	2.9	M		•			
Sprayed Cellulose							
Cellulose	3.5	M	•	•[3]			

[1] The foil facing on some batt and blanket insulation can serve as a vapor barrier only if the joints are taped adequately.

[2] Applies if the boards are faced with aluminum foil and all joints are taped or caulked.

[3] Spray cellulose limited to wall cavities.

[4] The claim that no separate vapor barrier is needed has not yet been universally accepted.

Air and Vapor Barriers

Thermal insulation reduces heat transfer by blocking conduction through the construction materials that make up wall and roof assemblies. Because the materials do not fit together perfectly, the inevitable gaps allow air to infiltrate, bypassing the insulation and leaking heat to the outdoors. Caulking and weatherstripping windows and doors go a long way to tighten the envelope against convective heat flow, but quality construction employs a second line of defense in the form of an **air barrier** material that wraps the house just under the exterior cladding.

So called "housewrap" materials let moisture escape but check air from infiltrating. It comes in rolls and is stapled to the sheathing. Joints are then taped with a plastic sealing tape (contractor's tape). Still, some experts think covering the entire wall surface is redundant, because only the joints leak air. They advise that taping only the joints and leaving the solid portions of the sheathing unwrapped makes an effective air barrier.

Conserving energy in the building envelope also requires keeping moisture out of the structure. When warm, moist air migrates through walls and roofs to the colder outdoors in winter, it condenses at some point along the path. Depending on where this occurs in the wall or roof, this moisture can cause insulation to lose efficiency, wood framing and sheathing to decay and outside paint to peel.

The accepted way to avoid these woes is to seal the envelope on the inside in regions where heating is the dominant need and on the outside in warm climates where air conditioning is the primary need. Sealing a house in either of these two ways yields a "tight" house that lacks sufficient fresh air for the occupants and combustion air for fuel-burning appliances. There are various ways to ensure an adequate supply of fresh air, such as heat recovery air-to-air heat exchangers and no house should be completely sealed without providing a compensating air supply. What about too little humidity for health and comfort? While some moisture in the air is necessary for health and well being, it will likely be retained in a tighter home.

The key to sealing the envelope is a good, continuous **vapor barrier** material with a low permeance rating, the index of a material's ability to block the passage of moisture. Polyethylene sheet and aluminum foil both have very low permeability to moisture and are adaptable to both new and existing construction. Even oil-base paint and shellac can be used, although oil-based paints may be increasingly scarce in the future. Vapor barriers are always recommended in cold climates to keep moisture out of the structure in winter. The barrier always goes between the insulation and heated space, usually just under the wall finish material. The reverse is true in warm humid climates (South Carolina, Georgia, Alabama, Florida, Louisiana, Mississippi and southern half of Texas), where the barrier goes near the outer surface, to keep the more humid outside air from entering the air-conditioned interior.

SOLAR HEAT AND LIGHT

The sun can be a constant source of free heat and light. It would be foolish not to use it, but only after paying due attention to energy conservation by sealing the building envelope against unwanted heat loss and gain. Far more solar energy falls on the surface of the earth than we need. Unfortunately, though the energy is free for the taking, capturing solar energy costs, as does storing it for when we need it. The energy crises of the 1970s spawned many technologies for using the sun's energy for heating, cooling, daylighting and electricity. Some of these fell by the wayside in the intervening years, because they were either too costly or complicated, combined with drops in energy prices and abandonment of governmental incentives.

Of the numerous devices invented to turn sunshine into useful home heat, the most cost-effective approaches to date have also been the simplest. They use the house itself to collect, distribute and store solar heat rather than depend on complicated systems of panels, pumps, distribution lines and controls. Windows are necessary in any case, so why not make them do double-duty to collect solar heat? You can do this by placing them on the south walls of the house, where they stand to gain the most useful solar heat on an annual basis.

Of course, heat gained by a south-facing window isn't always desirable and never desirable in areas needing cooling throughout the year. The trick to getting the windows to work for you is to provide some kind of control. Inside controls, such as blinds and drapes work to control light, but don't keep out much heat, because it has already penetrated the glass. Awnings or roof overhangs, mounted outside work best. A simple rule of thumb for sizing an overhanging awning or roof eave is as follows:

Horizontal overhang projection = window height x overhang factor

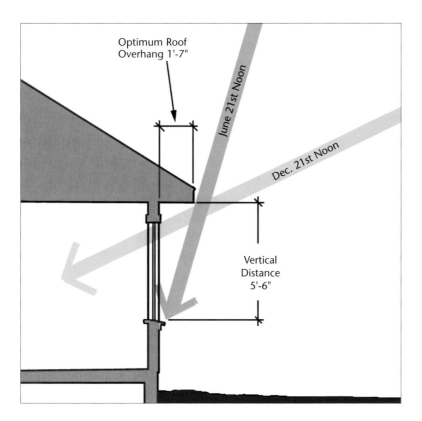

Optimum Roof Overhang 1'-7"

June 21st Noon

Dec. 21st Noon

Vertical Distance 5'-6"

Figure 4.4 You can get a good idea of the optimum overhang for summer shading and winter solar heat gain by multiplying the vertical distance shown here by the overhang factor in the table below.

The overhang projection and vertical distance to be used are shown in Figure 4.4. You can find the appropriate overhang factor by looking up your latitude on a map and matching it with the table below.

LATITUDE	Representative Location	Overhang Factor
28°	Tampa, Fla.; San Antonio, Texas	0.09
32°	San Diego, Calif.; Dallas, Texas	0.16
36°	Las Vegas, Nev.; Nashville, Tenn.	0.22
40°	Denver, Co.; Philadelphia, Pa.	0.29
44°	Boise, Idaho; Minneapolis, Minn.	0.37
48°	U.S./Canadian border, western	0.45
52°	Calgary, Regina	0.54

For example, if you want to find the overhang length for a south-facing kitchen window in Salt Lake City, you first determine that Salt Lake City is at North Latitude 32°. Your sill height above floor is 42 inches (1,067 mm)). If the eave height is 9 feet (108 inches, 2,743 mm) above the floor, you will have a vertical distance of 108 inches minus

42 inches (2,743 mm minus 1,067 mm), or 66 inches (1,676 mm) to enter in the formula. Your required overhang length will thus be 66 x 0.029 = 19 inches (1,676 mm x 0.029 = 483 mm). This rule of thumb is generally good for areas that can benefit from some solar heat. If you are located in a climatic zone that always needs cooling, such as south Florida, your overhangs should block as much of the sun as possible, year round.

Light from the sun, called "**daylighting**" by architects and engineers, is most always welcome in kitchens and baths, both for the free light it provides, but even more for the cheerful way it enlivens a room. Any plants used to enhance the space thrive better in natural light, as well. You can introduce solar light into a space from windows in any wall, regardless of their solar orientation, but the direction windows face does affect the type and amount of light you'll get, so heed the following guidelines:

South-facing windows	Get the most total light, year round. The light is direct when the sky is clear and glare is thus a problem. Protect against unwanted heat during warm seasons with the appropriate overhang or awning.
East-facing windows	Get early morning light, especially welcome in kitchens and dining nooks and desirable in baths. Except in warm climates, east-facing windows probably do not need shade protection.
West-facing windows	Get afternoon light, which unfortunately comes with unwanted heat during the summer. Shade trees of proper size and location provide the best control. In their absence, use vertical blinds or shutters, preferably mounted outside for warm season control of heat and glare.
North-facing windows	Only get direct sunlight in early morning and late afternoons in summer, in northern areas, but get diffuse daylight during the entire day in all seasons. While they are not cursed with glare and unwanted heat, north-facing windows are always a heat loss liability in the winter, so make sure you use energy-efficient windows and keep the total glass areas small.

The most recent breeds of "high-performance" windows contain improvements that make these guidelines less rigid than they are for standard single- and double-glazed windows, as we'll see in Chapter 9.

LET THE CLIMATE BE YOUR GUIDE

As you can see by now, designing an energy-efficient home is a hefty charge, involving knowledge of several types of windows. You can make sure the building envelope is energy-efficient by providing the proper amount of insulation and using efficient windows, then use the sun's energy as much as feasible for free heat and daylight. Because the outside climate differs region to region, your overall design strategy should use the seasonal features of your climate as a starting point for design. The map in Figure 4.5 divides the U.S. and Canada into seven major climatic regions. Following are the characteristics of each region and some energy-conserving design strategies. Check with your state energy code, if one exists, and local building department before applying the guidelines in your area.

Figure 4.5 The United States and Canada span several climate zones. Climate-responsive building design is achieved by using the appropriate guidelines for the zone.

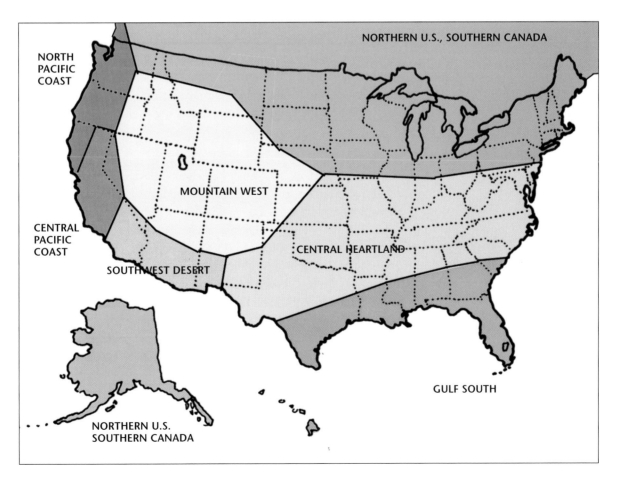

Northern U.S/Southern Canada

Summers are short and mostly pleasant in the band that stretches across the northern portion of the U.S. and Canada. Autumns can be spectacular. The downside is the cold, long winters that dominate the climate and are the major focus of energy-efficient design. Begin with a well-insulated envelope to keep heat loss to a minimum. Insulate roofs/ceilings to a minimum of R-38, walls and foundations to R-19 and floors above crawl spaces to R-19. If your project is an addition, try to shelter it from winter winds. Make sure the construction is well sealed against infiltration. Choose the most efficient windows (R-3 or better) and make generous use of south-facing windows to collect winter sun.

Mountain West

Dryness and abundant sunshine mark the climate of the western states that lie between the Sierra Nevadas and Great Plains. Numerous mountains, valleys and canyons create a variety of microclimates. Winters can be cold and stormy, with cold winds barreling down out of the northwest. In spring, winds often blast down out of canyons. The good news, outside of the dryness, is that the winters in this region are tempered by plentiful sunshine. Summers in the mountains are cool enough to require some heating throughout the year. Low-lying areas can be hot, but the low humidity and cool nights makes them bearable.

Start with a tight, well-insulated envelope. Insulate roof/ceilings to a minimum R-38, walls, foundations and floors above crawl spaces to R-19. Locations in the higher mountains or those prone to winter winds coming down out of the mountains should receive higher insulation levels. Orient the main windows southward to capitalize on solar heating. Massive interior materials such as tile-on-concrete floors and masonry walls can help both comfort and save energy by absorbing solar heat during the day and releasing it during the night. Protect windows with overhangs or plants against the strong summer sun and minimize glass on the west-facing side, if possible. Divert or screen winter winds by landscaping, but allow breezes to cool the interior in summer. In low-lying areas, plants and water adjacent to the outer walls can help cool the building in summer by evaporating water, thus cooling entering air.

North Pacific Coast

The rain, fog and steady Pacific breezes of the coastal zone west of the Cascades make for cool and gray conditions much of the year. Even so, this is an easy climate in which to design. In spite of the lack of sunshine, solar heating is worth the effort because so little heat is needed. Locate windows on the south to receive solar heat and use massive floors inside to absorb and store the energy. Cold, wet winds plague this region, so know where your winds come from and limit window areas facing this direction. Insulate roof/ceilings to R-38, walls, foundations and floors above crawl space to R-19. Provide adequate insulation and weatherstripping.

Central Pacific Coast

Hot dry summers and abundant sunshine mark the Mediterranean climate of California's Central Valley, which stretches from Oregon to Los Angeles. Winters are moderately rainy, colder in the north than south. Variations in elevation and proximity to mountains and sea create numerous microclimates.

We can learn much from the ranch houses, missions and adobes indigenous to this region. Long and low, with the long sides oriented towards the winter sun, their overhangs block summertime solar heat. Floors and interior walls are often masonry, which absorbs heat during the day to release it during the cooler night. Patios and courtyards offer outdoor living during the abundant periods of mild weather. Operable windows on upper and lower levels allow cooling breezes inside at night. If fences contain outdoor living spaces, they are held away from these windows so as not to block the ventilation. Insulate roof/ceilings to R-30, walls and foundations to R-19.

Southwest Desert

Vacationers and retirees flock to the desert climate of the Southwest in droves. They come for the warm, dry climate that prevails for most of the year. But many leave in summer when things get really hot. The searing temperatures of a summer day are often followed by a chilly night. Wide temperature swings combine with more sunshine than anywhere else in the U.S. to make this region the best location for solar heating. Massive construction materials should be used for floors and walls to store solar heat and balance the diurnal temperature extremes. Because of the dry air, evaporative (swamp) coolers can make the interiors more comfortable, except for the hottest part of summer, when mechanical air conditioning is the only means of achieving comfort. For insulation, provide levels of R-30 in roof/ceilings, R-19 in walls, R-11 in foundations.

Central Heartland

The region stretching westward from the mid-Atlantic coast to the plains of Texas and northward from the Gulf states to Great Lakes has a relatively temperate climate with four distinct seasons. Summers are hot and humid. Winters are mild along the Atlantic coast, colder farther inland. Rainfall, also heaviest along the Atlantic slope, prevails throughout the region. The ever-present winds sometimes become tornadoes or hurricanes in summer and fall. Climate-responsive design in this region starts with well-insulated walls and roofs. Insulate roof/ceilings to R-38, walls, foundations and floors above crawl space to R-19. Deploy windows to catch winter sun and cooling breezes in warm periods, but shield them from the summer sun and hurricane winds.

Gulf South

For most of the year heat and humidity dominate the coastal areas that lie on the Gulf of Mexico. Heavy rains and hurricane-force winds also plague the region. On the upside, very mild winters make the heating season short—even non-existent in Southern Florida. Sunlight is a liability in this region for most of the year, so windows should be placed for light, view and ventilation, rather than capturing solar heat. Provide them with roof overhangs or awnings to block unwanted heat and protected from both high winds and heavy rains. Exterior shutters that completely close over the windows are a good option here. Climate control is easier with an array of many smaller windows than a few large ones. Heavy wind damage incurred by homes in this region in recent years has resulted in stricter construction requirements. Before finalizing a design, find out from the local building department which requirements apply. Insulate roof/ceilings to R-30, walls to R-19 and foundations to R-19 except in southern Florida, where R-19 suffices. Floors need no insulation.

HVAC Systems

Even the most energy-conserving kitchen/bath won't likely get all of its heat or light from solar sources. The space will need mechanical or electrical heating or cooling at some times of the day or year to create comfort inside (you may not even get a building permit without a mechanical heating source).

The central heating/ventilating/air conditioning (HVAC) system must provide whatever auxiliary heating or cooling is required. If you are remodeling an existing room, the task of heating/cooling in the new configuration may be as simple as rerouting a few heat ducts or pipes. In an addition, you may be able to extend the heating system of the house into the new area if the location works out and the equipment has enough capacity.

The option gets less feasible as the size and complexity of the addition expands. The HVAC system of the home may not have additional capacity. And extending existing distribution piping or ducts may not be feasible. Controlling the amount of heat is a third obstacle. If the system is set up as a single zone that responds to a centrally located thermostat, adding an outward wing will require rethinking the entire system and possibly adding an extra zone.

If auxiliary HVAC equipment is needed, consult with a reliable heating/cooling contractor or mechanical engineer to review the options and select an appropriate unit. There's no advantage in installing equipment with more capacity than you actually need, so consult with your heating contractor or engineer as soon as you have a basic layout. The consultant will determine the necessary capacity and suggest system options based on the size of the area, placement of windows and amount of insulation. Because cabinets and fixtures occupy much of the floor space at the perimeter of kitchen and bath areas, be sure to coordinate the points of distribution with the consultant.

Appliances

The "bigger is better" ethic often prevails notwithstanding the fact that energy-efficient appliances have been available for years. But their market share has been scant due to higher initial cost, fewer options and smaller size. For example, consumers may prefer a refrigerator that dispenses ice and cold water to one that simply makes ice cubes in trays. Still, if you are concerned about an appliance's energy use, you can assess its efficiency from the **Energy Guide Label** affixed to the appliance. It will give numbers for an **energy efficiency rating (EER)** for appliances whose efficiency is independent of the climate, such as refrigerators. Appliances for which the season of the year is a variable, such as air conditioners, contain a **seasonal energy efficiency rating (SEER)**. In either case, the higher the number, the more efficient the appliance.

Incorporating energy efficiency into every aspect of your design work is the right thing to do. It's not only environmentally responsible, but allows you to create comfortable, functional, pleasant interior environments that will save your clients money over time.

PART TWO – THE BUILDING ENVELOPE

CHAPTER 5: The Forces on Houses

The most basic function of a house is shelter. But shelter from what? We have always expected our house to shelter us from snow, rain and wind. In modern times we have come to extend the concept of shelter to include shelter from the outside thermal extremes, be they freezing cold or searing heat. We can think of these climatic elements as forces that act upon the structure. The challenge for design then becomes finding ways to design the envelope to withstand the various forces that impinge upon it.

We've already been introduced to these *thermal forces* in Chapter 4, when we talked about energy-efficient design. But there are other forces that act on the structure and they push or pull on it in a *physical way*. Dealing with them is the focus of this chapter. The goal is not to turn you into a structural engineer, but to give you a basic overview of how both internal and external forces impose themselves on the house and the design strategies used to resist them.

INTERNAL FORCES

Architects and engineers classify the physical forces that act on a building as **loads**, then set out to design the structure to stand up under the maximum expected loads. **Dead loads** exert a constant force, whereas **live loads** impose themselves intermittently on the structure. Gravity is the source of both dead- and live-load forces. The materials that make up the structure all weigh something. Since these materials remain in place after assembly, their weights are considered as dead loads. Consider a bathroom floor, for example. The joists, subfloor and finish floor covering of a typical bathroom floor usually weigh in at around 10 pounds per square foot (psf) (0.479 kN/m^2) and joists can be sized from span tables that use these assumed dead-load weights. As a kitchen/bath designer you should be aware of special dead loads of any equipment included. For example, a bathtub-sized whirlpool can add 40 psf (1.92 kN/m^2) when filled to capacity, enough to require additional support in the form of larger joists, closer joist spacing or both.

Live loads are the weights of the things that move around on the structure—the occupants, their furniture and portable equipment. To eliminate the need for calculating the weight of every occupant, bed and sofa, these live-load items have been calculated for an average household and are specified in codes in pounds per square foot (psf).

Typical live loads for house floors are assumed at 40 psf (1.92 kN/m²), except attic floors used for storage only, for which 20 psf (0.96 kN/m²) usually suffices.

EXTERNAL FORCES

Houses must also withstand the physical forces nature imposes: wind, snow and earthquakes—all live loads—but in varying degrees, depending on the location.

Winds

Wind forces pose a design challenge in many parts of the U.S. and Canada and are practically negligible in other parts. The wind speed map in the *International Building Code* (IBC/2000) classifies design wind speeds into **basic speeds** and **three-second gusts**, listed as two numbers (85/38), where the higher one is the three-second gust. The lowest basic speed, 38 mph (61.2 km/h), is found along the West coast, including Washington, Oregon and California. As you might expect, the hurricane-prone coastal areas of the Gulf of Mexico incur the highest speeds, 67 mph (107.9 km/h) with gusts up to 150 mph (241.5 km/h). The Atlantic coastal areas are slightly better off with a basic speed of 40 mph (64.4 km/h) and gusts up to 90 mph 144.9 km/h), except for Cape Hatteras (140/63 mph) (225.4/101.4 km/h).

Residents of hurricane-prone regions of the U.S know first hand of the destructive potential of the high winds that come in the summer and fall. At a minimum, parts of buildings blow off, sometimes causing damage to other buildings or injuring people. At worst, hurricanes lift entire light-frame houses off their foundations. Each major event yields new information about the ability of materials and building techniques to withstand heavy winds and building officials incorporate this data into subsequent versions of the building codes. Armed with the latest guidelines for wind-resistant construction and good structural sense, there's no good reason we can't design and build houses to stand up to wind forces in even the most vulnerable regions.

Obtaining a sense for wind-resistant design calls for an understanding of how wind forces act on a house. The highest portion, the roof, is most vulnerable. Wind pushes against one (the positive) side and pulls on the other (negative) side. In pulling, wind exerts an upward suction on flat roofs and on the leeward side of sloped roofs. The pull, or suction, on overhangs is greater than on the roof itself and greatest on open porches. As you might expect, high buildings are more vulnerable to wind than low ones.

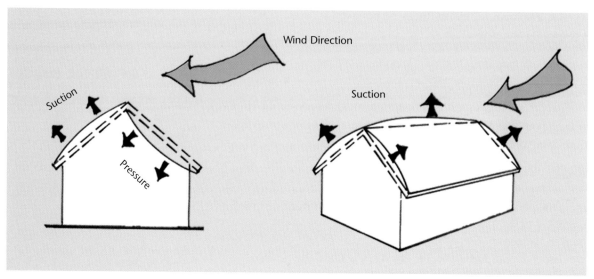

Figure 5.1 Wind blowing against the sloped side of a roof exerts pressure on the windward side and suction on the leeward side (left). Wind blowing against the gable end creates suction on the entire roof (right).

Wind also affects walls, pushing against walls perpendicular to the direction of the wind and wracking walls parallel to the wind, as shown in Figure 5.2. Walls containing a lot of glass are especially vulnerable, not only because of the glass itself, but also the fact that glass is an infill, rather than part of the structure. As such, it interrupts the continuity of the structure, creating a weak area requiring special design provisions.

Figure 5.2 Wind striking vertical surfaces tends to topple or wrack them as shown by the dotted lines. This effect can be countered by bracing the walls with panels or cross bracing.

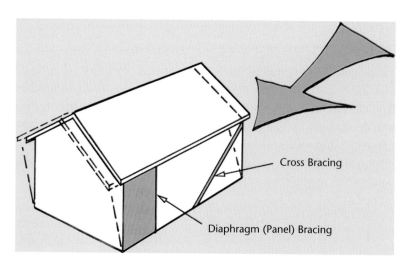

Designers counter wind forces on buildings in three ways:

- Select roofing and siding that will resist being blown or sucked off and attach it with proven methods. Wood and fiberglass shingles, for example, are more vulnerable than properly anchored tiles.

- Design walls to be stiff enough to resist perpendicular (head-on) winds, especially critical in walls containing a lot of glass.

- Brace roofs and walls to withstand the force of winds acting parallel to the structure. This usually takes the form of cross bracing in walls or solid panel sheathing in walls and roofs.

Seismic Forces

Seismic forces are those that arise from the earth to shake the building from below. But the damaged or collapsed buildings and fissures in the ground that we associate with seismic forces are only the results of the most intense earthquakes. Actually, the surface of the earth is constantly shifting to some degree, but we notice the movement only when it reaches the intensity of a tremor, temblor or earthquake.

The likelihood of serious seismic movement is greatest in mountainous areas, particularly those that are young in geological time. That's why the major events of the twentieth century—the 1906 earthquake in San Francisco and the 1989 Loma Prieta Earthquake—struck along fault lines near the coastal mountains of California. A 1959 earthquake near Yellowstone National Park caused a massive landslide that dammed up the Madison River and created an entirely new lake.

The National Oceanic and Atmospheric Administration charted the areas of earthquake hazard according to the potential for building damage (Figure 5.3). A far more extensive series of maps indicating seismic damage in terms of ground movement appear in the *International Building Code*. These maps form the basis for calculating the proper design for each region. While this method is beyond the scope of this book, there are some basic things you should know about seismic forces and houses.

41

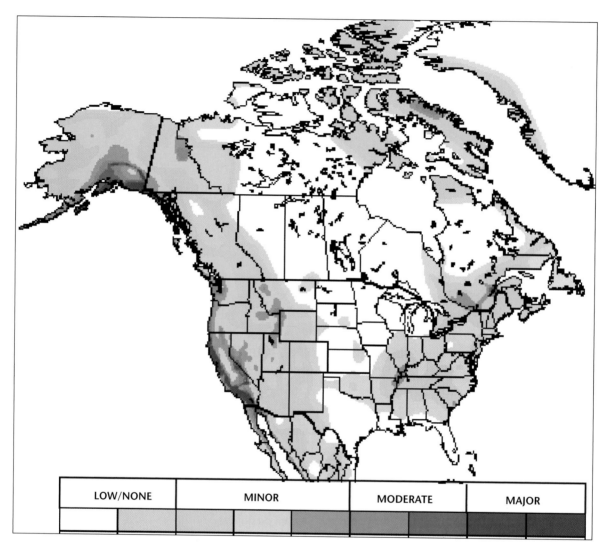

Figure 5.3 The potential earthquake damage in North America is greatest in the Rocky Mountains and Sierra Nevada Range, which are geologically new and unstable areas.

First, seismic forces tend to shake buildings apart and separate them from their foundations. Light-framed buildings are less prone to seismic damage—and easier to beef up to resist seismic forces—than heavy buildings made of masonry and/or concrete. Masonry buildings also create a greater hazard to people when components come loose in an earthquake.

Because seismic forces are lateral (horizontal), many of the same lateral bracing measures used to resist wind forces, such as cross bracing and panel sheathing, are effective.

In addition to proper lateral bracing, it is imperative to connect each component of the structure adequately to carry the seismic loads from the roof ridge down through the walls, foundation and into the ground. Connections in seismic-prone areas usually involve much more than simple nailing. Metal plates, ties and details all have their proper place. As a designer, find out from your building department the level of seismic severity of your region and which design measures are recommended in home design.

Snow Loads

Except for the southernmost parts most of the United States and Canada get enough snowfall to require it as a factor in roof design. Values given in the IBC/2000 code range upwards to 100 psf (4.79 kN/m²) for the contiguous states and Canada and up to 300 psf (14.37 kN/m²) in parts of Alaska. Many areas are noted as "case specific," with the design snow load values to be determined by local building officials. Snow is intermittent, hence a **live load**. The IBC makes allowances for the type of roof, amount of insulation, unequal loading, rain-on-snow surcharge and other factors. Find out the value to use from your local building department.

With a general understanding of the physical forces that a house must withstand, you will be a better qualified, more knowledgeable member of the building team.

CHAPTER 6: Foundations

Every house sits on some kind of foundation, which carries its weight and anchors it to the ground. The foundation may extend no deeper than necessary to prevent it from frost damage or deep enough to contain a basement. While most foundations are made of concrete or masonry, they can also be made of wood. In this chapter we'll scan the types of foundations you will most likely encounter in residential construction.

HOW DEEP A FOUNDATION?

The foundation of a home must be deep enough to:

1. Extend below the frost line.

2. Extend into solid bearing soil.

3. Provide space for mechanical or electrical equipment and/or utility or living space.

The requirement to extend below the frost line is to ensure that the foundation won't freeze. When concrete and masonry freeze they tend to crack, which reduces their structural capacity and creates pathways for water leakage. Section 1805 of the IBC/2000 requires that all footings for buildings larger than 400 square feet (36 m²) extend at least 12 inches (305 mm) below grade and also below the frost line "of the locality," leaving it up to designers to get this information from their local building department. Homes in Florida can get by with very shallow foundations. In New England, footings must extend down to four feet below grade. The *National Building Code of Canada* defines minimum foundation depth according to a table that includes factors such as soil type, drainage and whether the house sits over a heated or unheated basement/crawl space. Where it requires foundations to extend below the frost line, it leaves it up to "local experience" to determine the exact depth of the frost line.

Making sure the foundation extends into solid bearing material is more complicated. Soils vary greatly in their ability to support imposed loads. Soils rich in organic material, such as topsoils, will give way under any load. Clays are iffy. Loams and mixed soil are better, gravel better still and rock best. Bearing values, according to

IBC/2000 vary from 1,500 psf (71.85 kN/m^2) for clay types to 12,000 psf (574.8 kN/m^2) for crystalline bedrock. If there is any doubt as to the type of soil, either assume the lowest value or have the soil tested by a qualified firm.

Not all homes need space below the first floor to house equipment or storage. Furnaces, air conditioners, water heaters and pumps can all be housed above grade if provisions are made for their distribution systems and certain other details accommodated. For example, fresh air intake and exhaust provisions must be made for heating/ventilating equipment. Ducts and water pipes in attic spaces must be insulated. Noise must be isolated.

Homeowners use basements primarily to store seldom-used items and sometimes finish off certain areas for living space. As with mechanical/electrical equipment, these functions can most often be accommodated on an aboveground floor. All homes need some storage space and because basements are usually as large as the floor above, they can store a lot. Living space below grade is sometimes advantageous, particularly if the house sits on a slope that allows the basement rooms to open onto the outdoors for access, light and view. But moisture must be dealt with in all below-grade construction, as we'll see later.

Shallow Foundations

Getting to and from below-grade space requires stairs and with an aging population, we can safely expect more homes in the future to be built without basements. Houses without basements often rest on grade-beam foundations consisting of a concrete slab floor thickened at the outer perimeter. The slab portion consists of cast-in-place concrete, usually four inches thick and reinforced with wire mesh. The thickened outer edge—or grade-beam—contains horizontal reinforcing bars placed in the top and bottom to make it strong enough to distribute the weight of the walls of the structure onto the soil without breaking apart. Grade-beam foundations go up quickly and economically, but come with some drawbacks. Mechanical, electrical and plumbing distribution systems should, where possible, be installed in ceilings or walls, rather than below the slab, where they are more easily accessible for repairs or future alterations.

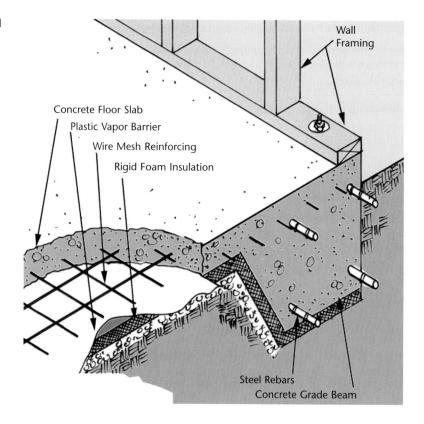

Figure 6.1 Components of a typical grade-beam foundation.

Wall Framing

Concrete Floor Slab

Plastic Vapor Barrier

Wire Mesh Reinforcing

Rigid Foam Insulation

Steel Rebars

Concrete Grade Beam

Crawl Space Foundations

If the homeowner doesn't need a full basement for storage or mechanical equipment, the extra expense and potential problems that may arise from a deep basement can be eliminated by a shallow or "crawl space" foundation. In cold regions, footings are required to go down just below the frost line, which is always less than required for a full basement. While the space between the ground and the first floor isn't sufficient for storage, it provides a useful area in which to run pipes, wires and ducts. There is nevertheless one downside compared to a full-basement: no space for traditional furnaces or water heaters.

Crawl space foundations typically consist of concrete or masonry walls set on continuous concrete footings, though wood may also be used, as we'll see later on. Because this type of foundation needs no floor for walking on, the grade is the floor and presents two problems. Moisture wicking up through the soil can damage any wood above and carries pathogens such as radon and mold. Also, rodents can easily burrow into the house through an earth floor. There are two ways to address these concerns. The more expensive way is to pour a concrete "rat" slab over a poly vapor barrier. The slab doesn't have to be troweled smooth, as in a basement, since it is not intended for an occupied space. The second, more economical approach is to simply lay a 6-mil poly vapor barrier over the soil, with seams overlapped and taped and edges taped to the foundation wall or run up the wall and sealed to the sill plate. This approach keeps moisture out of the crawl space but does not prevent entry of rodents.

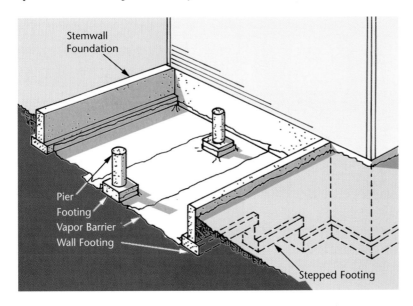

Figure 6.2 A crawl space foundation is bounded by a foundation just deep enough to extend below the frost line. A continuous vapor barrier is necessary to prevent ground moisture from wicking up into the space and damaging the wood floor framing above.

Full Basement Foundations

Houses with basements require continuous wall foundations between the main structure and ground. The foundations must carry the vertical load of the building to the footings while withstanding the horizontal forces of the earth and resisting penetration of water and moisture. Foundations in cold climates should be insulated, either on the outside or inside. Foundations are erected upon continuous footings that run below the foundation walls and are wide enough to distribute the building loads into the soil. The floor inside usually consists of a concrete slab, isolated from the ground with an impermeable poly vapor barrier. Well-designed foundation-footing systems contain gravel or a permeable mat next to the outer wall to relieve water pressure and conduct it downward. Perforated pipes are placed next to the footing to collect the water and conduct it away from the foundation.

Figure 6.3 A full basement foundation can be insulated on the outside or inside. In both cases, provisions should be made to allow surface water to drain down the outside of the wall and into a foundation drain, which empties onto grade, if slope permits, or into a sump pump.

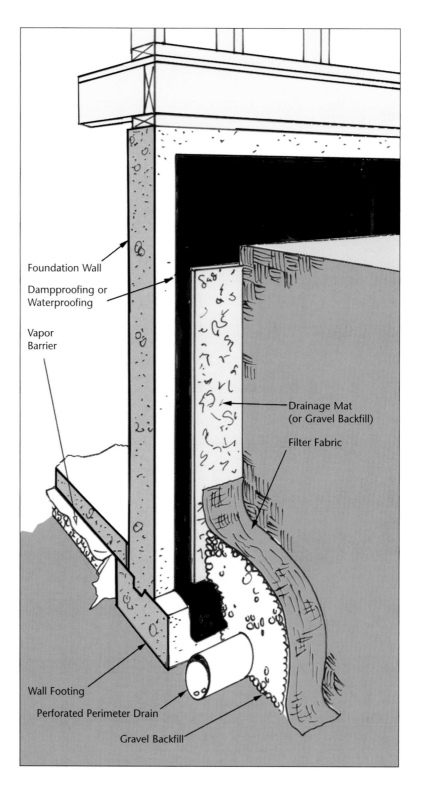

Foundation Wall

Dampproofing or Waterproofing

Vapor Barrier

Drainage Mat (or Gravel Backfill)

Filter Fabric

Wall Footing

Perforated Perimeter Drain

Gravel Backfill

Pier Foundations

Sometimes the house or portion of a house is disconnected from the grade completely, which reduces the foundation cost while eliminating the problems of soil-borne moisture getting into the superstructure. Instead of resting on a full foundation, the structure bears on an array of piers or posts. This method is not only the most common way to support porches and decks, but also suits certain room additions. One tradeoff for the cost savings is the appearance. A house on stilts may look right by the seashore but out of place in an urban or suburban setting. Another downside is the loss of a contained space below the floor to house equipment or run pipes and ducts. But if they are well insulated, pipes and ducts can be located within the floor structure. Post and pier supports must bear on concrete footings properly sized to distribute their weight onto the soil without sinking.

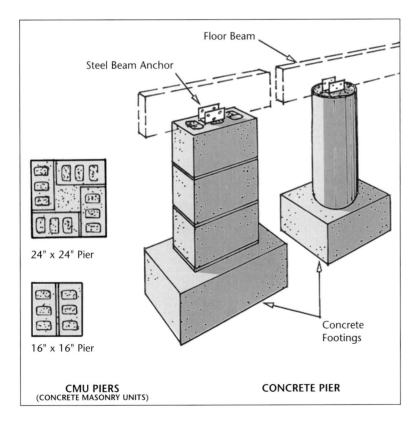

Figure 6.4 Piers may be used as the entire foundation in some cases or as supports within an exterior foundation wall in others. Concrete blocks or poured concrete are two favorite means of constructing the piers.

FOUNDATION MATERIALS

Any material used for exterior walls below grade must withstand the vertical forces of the building, the horizontal forces of the earth and resist water, a tall order. Fortunately, there are several materials proven to meet the challenge. Each has its own opportunities and limitations.

Poured Concrete

Long life, structural stability, strength and resistance to water have made poured-in-place concrete the most used material for below-grade construction. To perform up to its potential, however, concrete must be mixed with the proper ratio of water, gravel, sand and cement, poured without delay, then kept from freezing in cold weather and drying out too rapidly in hot weather while it cures. Reinforcement of some sort is always required. The minimum requirements for simple, uncomplicated foundation walls are obtainable from the local building department. Qualified specialists should design more complicated walls.

Concrete foundations have traditionally been poured into wood forms that must first be erected and braced, then taken down after the concrete has cured. The recent trend toward more energy-efficient construction has generated a new technique that incorporates foam plastic insulation into the forms. The forms then remain in place to insulate the wall. There are a variety of such systems currently in use, called by various names, "permanent insulated formwork," "cast-in-place foundation systems" and "insulated concrete foundations" (ICFs). All rely on expanded polystyrene (EPS, or "beadboard") foam as the base material and contain vertical and horizontal cavities in which to run reinforcing steel.

Figure 6.5 Concrete forms are increasingly giving way to insulated concrete forms (ICFs) made of rigid foam, which both form the wall and remain in place to insulate afterward. Several systems are available. The one shown employs galvanized steel webs to hold the two sides of the forms in place. Mounting plates at the surface allow the attachment of framing or wall materials.

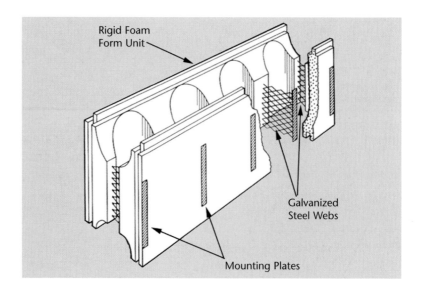

Rigid Foam
Form Unit

Galvanized
Steel Webs

Mounting Plates

Concrete Block

Many houses in North America sit on foundations made of concrete block. Traditional block foundations consist of modular blocks laid one by one in a bed of mortar. Steel reinforcing is required both vertically and horizontally, as determined by the local code. Ladder-shaped wire mesh is often used in horizontal joints, while steel rebars that extend from the footing up through the cores of the block form the vertical reinforcement.

Surface bonding (also called dry setting), a faster, easier method of joining concrete blocks, has been gaining ground in recent years. Rather than laying blocks, one by one, in mortar joints, they are simply stacked on each other. Both faces are then coated with a pre-packaged surface-bonding mix composed of Portland cement, sand and chopped fiberglass, which locks the blocks tightly together. Because both faces are coated, a separate application of mortar to the wall is not required for waterproofing, as it is with mortar-set blocks. Cores to receive vertical reinforcing bars still have to be filled with mortar however, as with blocks set in mortar joints.

Both mortar-set and surface-bonded block foundations can be insulated on either face, as with poured concrete, or by loose fill poured into the cores of the block. Special blocks containing built-in foam insulation are also available.

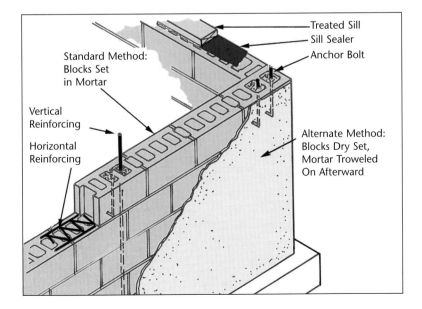

Figure 6.6 Concrete block foundations are traditionally laid up in mortar, but can also be constructed by setting the blocks on each other without mortar, then applying mortar to the interior and exterior face (surface bonding).

Wood Foundations

Wood, a most unlikely foundation material, has nonetheless been used successfully for the foundations of thousands of homes. Though "all weather wood foundations" are not accepted by all local codes, they have certain advantages over concrete. They go up faster and can be erected by carpenters. Because wood is an organic, renewable material, as opposed to concrete, which requires very high amounts of energy to manufacture, wood foundations also rate better than concrete or masonry, when environmental concerns are considered. Wood foundations, like wood studwalls, contain cavities that are easily insulated. To perform well, a wood foundation must be constructed to tight specifications, available from the National Forest Products Association (NFPA). Lumber must be pressure treated or of a naturally rot-resistant species such as clear heart cedar, redwood or cypress. Nails must be stainless steel. Wood foundations rest on footings of granular fill (coarse gravel), rather than concrete. Framed with 2x6 or 2x8 studs and plates, wood foundations are clad on the outside with pressure-treated plywood sheathing. Walls are built on the ground in 8-foot wide sections and then tilted up into place over the gravel footing. Once in place, the outside of the wall can be covered, damp-proofed or waterproofed and backfilled. The cavities can be insulated and enclosed. If there is a full basement, the finish can be applied directly to the studs of the foundation.

Figure 6.7 All wood foundations consist of pressure-treated wood framing set on a compacted gravel footing. If there is no slab on grade, a continuous moisture barrier is necessary to keep soil moisture from entering the crawl space or basement.

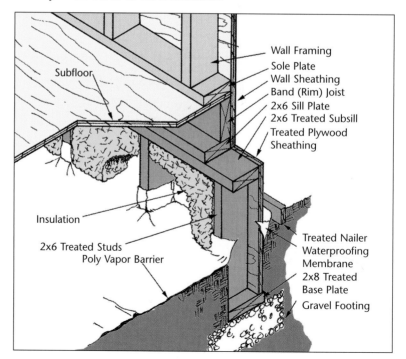

Subfloor

Insulation

2x6 Treated Studs
Poly Vapor Barrier

Wall Framing
Sole Plate
Wall Sheathing
Band (Rim) Joist
2x6 Sill Plate
2x6 Treated Subsill
Treated Plywood
Sheathing

Treated Nailer
Waterproofing
Membrane
2x8 Treated
Base Plate
Gravel Footing

CHAPTER 7: Floors

To reliably support the occupants and their household goods, floors must be designed as strong, durable platforms. Most residential floors consist of a wood or steel structural system with plywood or oriented strand board (OSB) subfloor. Concrete floor systems are the second most popular type. This chapter will help you grasp the basics of each system so you can confidently deal with the issues that arise in the course of the design and construction processes.

FLOOR FRAMING MATERIALS

A wood- or steel-framed floor system consists of three basic parts. From the top down, they are:

- Finish surface—the floorcovering and underlayment

- Subfloor or deck

- Joists which span between supports

The joists span between foundation walls or—more often—between an outside foundation wall and one or more beams that run parallel to the foundation. Beams, in turn, bear on internal bearing walls or columns.

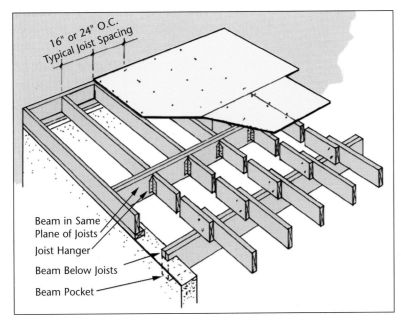

16" or 24" O.C.
Typical Joist Spacing

Beam in Same Plane of Joists
Joist Hanger
Beam Below Joists
Beam Pocket

Figure 7.1 A typical wood-framed floor consists of joists that span between the foundation walls and over any interior beams. Joists can either run over the tops of the beams or frame into them flush, attached by metal joist hangers. Plywood or OSB should always run with the long dimension perpendicular to the joists.

Keeping abreast with floor framing systems is harder today than it used to be, thanks to the many new materials at our disposal. As the quality of sawn lumber continues to decline, new materials come along to replace it, often with superior performance. Examples include lightweight steel framing and composition wood of various types, used in a variety of joists and beams. Nevertheless, sawn lumber is still in wide use in most residential floors, so it is important to understand the basics of the material.

Lumber Basics

The term "sawn lumber" includes a wide class of softwood milled to standard sizes and shapes. **Structural lumber** bears a grade stamp that indicates its stress rating. It includes shapes two or more inches in nominal thickness and width, suitable for joists, planks, beams, stringers, posts and timbers. With the exception of joists and planks, structural lumber is at least five inches in one dimension.

We get the softwood lumber from conifer trees such as pine, fir, hemlock and spruce. The terms "hardwood" and "softwood" are somewhat arbitrary, since some softwoods are harder than some hardwoods and vice versa. Still, the labels are useful to differentiate lumber according to end use. Softwoods are mostly used for structural purposes, while hardwoods end up in finish materials, cabinets and furniture.

Lumber Cuts. The cells that carry water and nutrients up and down in the trunk of the tree while it is growing comprise the fibers that give wood its structural strength. Just under the bark are active fiber cells—sapwood—that carries nutrients to the leaves. Sapwood cells are added faster during the warm than cool seasons, creating annular growth rings that show up as grain on the lumber. Inactive cells at the core comprise the heartwood, the darker portion of the cross-section of the log. How pieces are cut from this cross section affect qualities such as grain, texture, color, workability, stability and resistance to decay.

How boards are sliced from logs affects the grain pattern and tendency to deform. Lumber cut by slicing a log with parallel cuts is called "flat sawn" or "slash grained" in softwoods and "plain sawn" in hardwoods. The grain pattern varies from wide and wavy at the outer slices to narrow and vertical at slices near the center. Lumber cut perpendicular to the rings is termed "vertical grain" or "edge grained" in softwoods; "quarter sawn" in hardwoods. This cut yields a thin, vertical grain pattern with boards more dimensionally stable and warp-resistant than flat sawn boards.

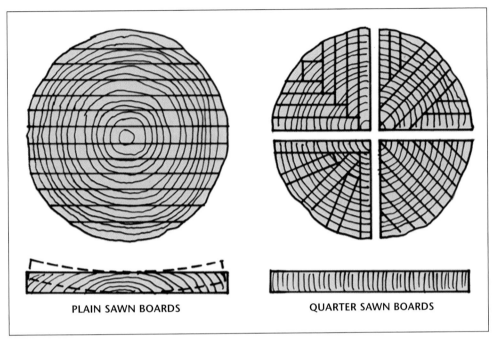

PLAIN SAWN BOARDS   **QUARTER SAWN BOARDS**

Moisture Content. All wood cut from living trees contains moisture—as much as 20% of the total weight. Exposing it to air (seasoning it) or heating it in a kiln removes some of the moisture, leaving it stiffer, stronger and less prone to shrinkage than green wood. Wood used for exterior framing and finish work should have a maximum 19% moisture content. Interior wood moisture content should not exceed 10 – 12%. Higher moisture content causes internal stresses in the wood that check, cup and warp it. Softwoods generally shrink more than hardwoods.

Figure 7.2 Plain sawn boards are sliced in parallel planes from the log, whereas quarter sawn boards are cut perpendicular to the growth rings.

Grading. Imperfections such as cupping, warping and knots make wood harder to cut, shape and build in straight and true assemblies. Trade associations develop and maintain grading standards which rate lumber according to the extent of its imperfections. Building codes typically require that all lumber and wood-based panels used for structural purposes bear the grade stamp of an approved grading agency and building inspectors look for grading stamps as a way of knowing whether the lumber is up to the task. Grade stamps look confusing at first, but once you crack the code, they tell you important qualities to look for, such as the grade of the lumber, species, moisture content, source mill and grading agency. Data for the following charts was obtained from American Softwood Lumber Standard, U.S. D.O.C. PS 20-70.

Lumber Grading Standards			
Grade	**Category**	**Dimension (nominal)**	**Use**
CONST (construction) **STAND** (standard) **UTIL** (utility)	Light framing	2 to 4 in. thick, 2 to 4 in. wide	Where high strength not required
SEL STR (select structural), **#1 & BTR** (#1 and better), **#1, #2, #3**	Structural light framing	2 to 4 in. thick, 2 to 4 in. wide	Trusses, tall concrete forms and where higher strength needed
SEL STR (select structural), **#1, #2, #3**	Structural joists and planks	2 to 4 in. thick, 5 in. and wider	Floor and ceiling joists, rafters
STUD	Stud	2 to 4 in. thick, 2 in. and wider	Studs of 10 ft. or less. Suitable for load-bearing walls

Figure 7.3 If you learn to read lumber grading stamps, you can obtain many facts pertaining to the source, grade, moisture content and species of the lumber.

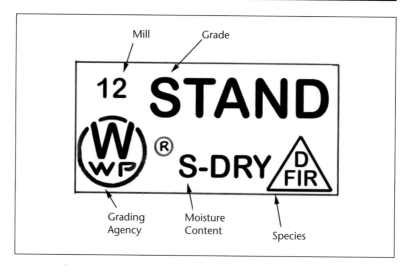

The standard for grading Canadian lumber is the *Standard Grading Rules for Canadian Lumber*, published by the National Lumber Grades Authority (NLGA). These standards meet those of the U.S. and grades and sizes of lumber in Canada are identical to those in use in the U.S.

Sizes. Softwood lumber is sold either by the lineal foot or board foot. One board foot represents a piece whose nominal size is one foot square by one inch thick. For example, a lineal foot of 2x12 contains two board feet. Boards are cut in the sawmill to their true-size dimensions, seasoned, then milled to their final dimensions, which trim off 1/4 or 1/2 inch. A 2x4, for example, emerges with final dimensions of 1 1/2 inches x 3 1/2 inches.

56

Moisture Content of Graded Lumber	
Moisture Content Indication	**Elaboration**
S-GRN	Surfaced while green. The moisture content when the lumber was planed exceeded 19%.
S-DRY	Surfaced while dry. The moisture content when the lumber was planed was 19% or less.
KD-19 or KD	The lumber has been dried in a kiln to a moisture content of 19% or less.
MC-15 or KD-15	The lumber has been dried to a moisture content of 15% or less.

Sizes of Milled Lumber			
Thickness		**Face Widths**	
Nominal	Actual (seasoned)	Nominal	Actual (seasoned)
1	3/4	2	1 1/2
1 1/4*	1	3	2 1/2
1 1/2**	1 1/4	**4**	**3 1/2**
2	1 1/2	5	4 1/5
2 1/2	2	**6**	**5 1/2**
3	2 1/2	7	6 1/2
3 1/2	3	**8**	**7 1/4**
4	3 1/2	9	8 1/4
		10	**9 1/4**
		11	10 1/4
		12	**11 1/4**

*Sometimes called "five quarters" and written 5/4.
**Sometimes called "six quarters" and written 6/4.
Sizes indicated in bold face type are those most readily available.

Engineered Lumber

Trees are a renewable resource, yet the rate of replacement hasn't kept up with the demand. The result is that younger trees are cut and the lumber has more checks, warps and knots than older growth trees. Among the alternative products have come along to take up the slack is "engineered" or "manufactured" lumber, made by bonding wood fibers or flakes together with resins under heat and high pressure. The resulting structural shapes have many advantages over sawn lumber:

- Longer lengths. Because joists and beams are made in a continuous process, lengths are limited only by shipping constraints. If a floor is 30 feet wide, you can get 30-foot long joists to span the distance without intermediate supports.

- Less moisture. With about half the moisture content of sawn lumber, engineered lumber shrinks less after installation. Floor joists won't shrink and cause squeaky floors when the heat is turned on.

- Uniform sizes and shapes. Joists and beams don't deform by checking, cupping and warping.

- Randomized defects. Instead of large knots that go completely through the member, reducing its strength, knots in engineered lumber are as thin as the layer in which they occur and are more random in location.

- Lighter weight. Engineered lumber is made in the most efficient structural shapes for the intended uses, with the result that they support the same loads with less material than sawn lumber.

- Holes for ducts and pipes. Larger diameter holes can be cut through manufactured joists than through standard lumber. Pre-punched cutouts are even provided in some members.

Engineered lumber is made by various processes. One consists of veneers glued together similar to plywood, except that the grain of each ply runs along the long length of the member and is called **laminated veneer lumber** or **LVL**. LVL is made into rectangular beams and I-shaped joists. Another process arranges wood fibers to run in the same directions, as they do in sawn lumber. The resulting **parallel strand lumber** yields long, straight beams, posts and studs. The third main type of engineered lumber consists of solid 2x4s or 2x6s glued together to form beams, called **glue-laminated beams**, or **glue-lams**.

Engineered lumber components install with standard carpentry tools and methods and are secured with nails, screws and bolts, but each product has certain limitations. When specifying these products, become familiar with the manufacturer's recommendations and incorporate them into the design.

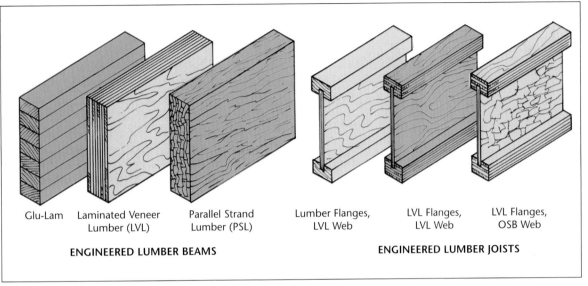

Glu-Lam Laminated Veneer   Parallel Strand   Lumber Flanges,   LVL Flanges,   LVL Flanges,
         Lumber (LVL)   Lumber (PSL)   LVL Web   LVL Web   OSB Web

ENGINEERED LUMBER BEAMS   **ENGINEERED LUMBER JOISTS**

Figure 7.4 Some of the types of engineered lumber beams and joists currently available as alternatives to sawn lumber, which is increasing in cost while declining in quality.

Using Tables to Size and Space Joists

Nominally 2-inch-thick sawn lumber continues to make up most joists that span 12 feet (3,658 mm) or less, so if you design floor systems, you should be able to select lumber joists from tables. First determine the span of the joists, then the live and dead loads the floor must support. Most codes require a minimum live load of 40 psf (1.92 kN/m²) for occupied rooms. As for dead loads, most residential floors weigh in at around 5 to 7 psf (0.24 to 0.34 kN/m²) for the framing and subfloor. Tile set in mortar adds around 20 psf (0.96 kN/m²), assuming an average 2-inch thickness and spas can add 60 psf (2.87 kN/m²) or more when full of water. Get exact weights from the supplier.

Next, you must decide how much deflection or "give" you will accept in the floor. Deflection is the distance the joists will sag at the mid point when the floor is fully loaded. It is limited to 1/360 of the joist span (written as l/360) if the floorcovering or ceiling below is a rigid material such as plaster or drywall that will crack when flexed. Deflection for all other floors is limited to 1/240. Still, many designers limit deflection to 1/360 because occupants don't like springy or bouncy floors.

You can now go to a joist span table to see what your options are. Regional lumber trade associations publish span tables for the species of lumber produced in their region. Similarly, manufacturers of engineered lumber publish span tables for their products.

Let's take an actual example. Say you have a kitchen addition that extends 14 feet beyond the main house and is 24 feet long. A full basement is to be added under the addition and the customer doesn't want the space encumbered with supporting posts. The most obvious solution is to select joists that span out over the 14 feet to bear on the new foundation.

Use a book of span tables to find possible joists and spacings. Find the table that applies to a floor with a 40-psf live load (the load for occupied rooms). The table, "Solid Lumber Floor Joists," is one such table, excerpted from *Maximum Spans: Southern Pine Joists & Rafters*, published by the Southern Pine Marketing Council.

Solid Lumber Floor Joists									
Southern Pine, 40 psf live load, 10 psf dead load, l/360									
Size	Spacing (inches on center)	Grade and Spacing (feet and inches)							
		Select Struct.	Non-Dense Select Struct.	No.1 Dense	No.1	No.1 Non-Dense	No.2 Dense	No.2	No.2 Non-Dense
2x6	12	11-2	10-11	11-2	10-11	10-9	10-11	10-9	10-3
	16	10-2	9-11	10-2	9-11	9-9	9-11	9-9	9-4
	24	8-10	8-8	8-10	8-8	8-6	8-8	8-6	8-2
2x8	12	14-8	14-5	14-8	14-5	14-2	14-5	14-2	13-6
	16	13-4	13-1	13-4	13-1	12-10	13-1	12-10	12-3
	24	11-8	11-5	11-8	11-5	11-3	11-5	11-0	10-6
2x10	12	18-9	18-5	18-9	18-5	18-0	18-5	18-0	17-3
	16	17-0	16-9	17-0	16-9	16-5	16-9	16-1	15-3
	24	14-11	14-7	14-11	14-7	14-0	14-0	13-2	12-6
2x12	12	22-10	22-5	22-10	22-5	21-11	22-5	21-9	20-11
	16	20-9	20-4	20-9	20-4	19-11	20-4	18-10	18-2
	24	18-1	17-9	18-1	17-5	16-8	16-8	15-4	14-10

You can see from the table that there are several possibilities, depending on the grade, size of the joist and spacing:

2x8 No. 2, spaced at 12 inches on center

2x10 No. 2 Dense, spaced at 24 inches on center

2x10 No. 2 Non-Dense, spaced at 16 inches on center

2x12 No. 2 Non-Dense, spaced at 24 inches on center

Now let's check the table, "Engineered Lumber Floor Joists (I-Joists)," to see how these possibilities compare with I-joists, for the same loading and deflection.

Engineered Lumber Floor Joists (I-Joists) 40 psf live load, 10 psf dead load, 1/360					
Depth (in.)	Spacing (in.)	Span (ft.-in.)	Depth (in.)	Spacing (in.)	Span (ft.-in.)
9 1/2	12	18-2	11 7/8	12	21-9
	16	16-6		16	19-9
	19.2	15-6		19.2	18-6
	24	14-4		24	17-1
	32	17-1		32	14-4

You could choose between 9 1/2-inch deep I-joists spaced at 24 inches or 11 7/8 inch joists spaced at 32 inches.

You might next use the desired joist depth to narrow the field. For example, if you want to match the depth of the 2x10 floor joists of the main house, your choices of solid lumber decrease to two and your options for I-joists to one (the 9 1/2-inch-deep one). The final choice might be made on economics. Fewer joists will be required if spaced 24-inches on center than if set 12 or 16 inches apart. But costs saved must be compared to the higher cost of thicker subfloor, required to span a greater distance. Plywood and OSB span ratings for subfloor are 16 and 24 inches on center, depending on the thickness.

Supporting the Joists

Joists bear onto walls or beams (girders), which must be designed to accept the accumulated loading of all joists that frame into them. In the example used above, the joists span between a ledger board attached to the band joist and a new foundation wall, so no intermediate beams are necessary. If one were, such as is usually required down the center of a full-wide basement, it could consist of multiple members of solid lumber or engineered lumber, or a steel beam. Sizing beams requires knowledge of structural theory beyond the scope of this book. If and when you need to select beams, get help from an architect or structural engineer.

Joists can connect to beams by running over their tops or by "flush framing" into their face. Flush framing is used when it is necessary to achieve maximum headroom below. Metal joist hangers are the preferred method of attaching joists to beams or girders in flush framing. A wide variety is available to suit the joist size and loading.

Framing Bumpout Floors

Bumping out the walls of a kitchen or bath without expanding the foundation can yield a few more feet of space. While this wouldn't mean much to a living room, the few extra feet in a small kitchen or bath might expand the planning options substantially. A tub might be placed in a bumpout, for example. Bumping out the floor parallel to the existing floor joists can be done by first removing the band joist in the bumpout area and attaching, or "scabbing" sister joists onto the main joists, with the outside ends cantilevering out over the foundation. Limit the overhang to 1/4 of the total length of the sister joists (for new floors, simply run the joists out 1/4 of the total span of the joist between supports). To bump part of the floor out perpendicular to the floor joists, extend the cantilever joists into the normal floor framing at least two joist bays into a doubled joist header and limit the amount of overhang to 24 inches (610 mm), unless an architect or engineer has designed the system.

Figure 7.5 Bumpouts can frame in either direction, with respect to the floor joists. Limit the projection to 24 inches when framing perpendicular to the joists and 1/4 of the joist span when framing parallel, unless the system is engineered.

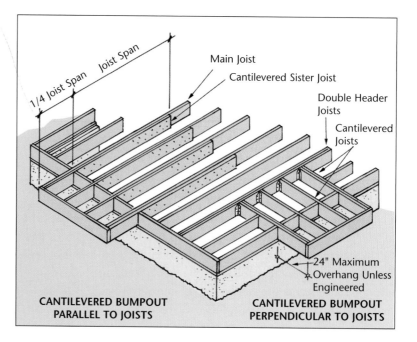

LIGHTWEIGHT STEEL-FRAMED FLOORS

Lightweight steel studs and joists, long used in commercial buildings, are becoming another increasingly popular alternative to sawn lumber in home construction. Steel floor joists are cold formed from galvanized sheet steel in various thicknesses, or gauges, then formed into structural shapes. They are made in lengths up to 40 feet. They have several advantages over sawn lumber:

- Pound for pound, steel is much stronger than wood.

- They are perfectly true and straight, free of checks, warps and knots.

- Moisture does not cause steel to swell or move.

- Steel joists offer a choice of stiffness for a given depth.

The main disadvantage is that the carpenters who install joists on houses may not be familiar with the special techniques and tools required for steel and must adapt to cutting with tin snips or a metal-cutting power saw and joining members with sheet metal screws.

Steel joists are C-shaped, in gauges of 18, 16, 14 and 12. Flanges vary from 2 inches to 3 1/2 inches (51 mm to 89 mm) in width. Standard depths are 6, 8, 10, 12 and 14 inches (152, 203, 254, 305 and 356 mm). Some come with pre-punched cutouts in their webs to allow wiring and piping to pass through (plastic grommets must be snapped into wiring holes to prevent the sheet metal from cutting into the wiring insulation).

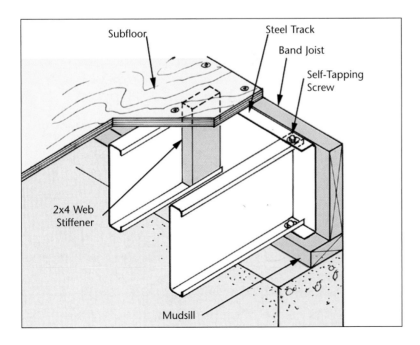

Figure 7.6 Lightweight steel joists are increasingly used alternatives to wood. A wood band (rim) joist provides a way to attach wall sheathing and siding.

Subfloor

Steel Track

Band Joist

Self-Tapping Screw

2x4 Web Stiffener

Mudsill

FLOOR TRUSSES

The maximum spans are limited for all joists, regardless of the material. For example, the longest span of a Southern Pine 2x12 spaced 16 inches (406 mm) on center is 21'-1" (6.42 m), for a standard 40 psf (1.92 kN/m²) live load. But this is for the best grade—dense select structural. If you got the worst grade, #3, the maximum span drops to 14'-5" (4.39 m). Reducing the spacing to 12 inches on center (o.c.) (305 mm) increases the span, but also ups the cost. Wood I-joists get spans up to 26 feet (7.92 m) and have other advantages over lumber, as described previously.

Today's larger homes often need clear spans greater than are practical with solid joists. Spans up to around 35 feet (10.66 m) are feasible with floor trusses. Trusses consist of continuous horizontal members, or chords, held apart by a series of short struts (web members) arranged in triangles. The assembly makes the best use of a given amount of material to distribute the vertical loads to the supports. Ducts and pipes can be run through the spaces in the web, whereas holes must be cut in solid joists and the size and location of the holes are restricted. Residential floor trusses typically use 2x4s for the top and bottom chords and wood or steel web members. Depths vary from 12 to 24 inches (305 to 610 mm). Trusses are expensive and have one other drawback—they must be ordered to exact length and cannot be altered on the job.

Figure 7.7 Several types of floor trusses make large spans possible without intermediate supports. Wiring, ducts or piping can be run through the spaces between web (triangulating) members.

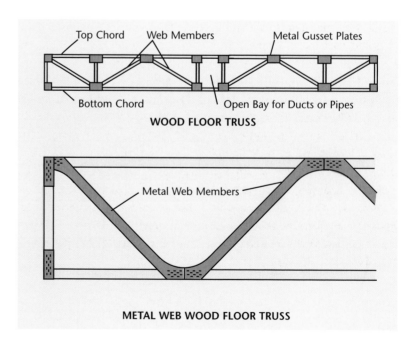

WOOD FLOOR TRUSS

METAL WEB WOOD FLOOR TRUSS

When designing upgrades to existing kitchen and bath floors, you may encounter floors too uneven or out of level to accept a new floorcovering. Or the supporting structure may be rotted from years of exposure to moisture. Even if the floor is sound, it might need modification for re-routing piping for plumbing fixtures or to support a spa. If the floor sits above a cold crawl space, it will need insulation to conserve heat and keep pipes from freezing. Depending on what's there and what's required for the proposed changes, the work can be as minor as modifying the finish surface or as major as ripping out the floor completely and installing new joists, subfloor, underlayment and floorcovering.

Upgrading a Wood Floor Structure

The framing that supports a floor may require any of the following improvements in a remodeling project:

- Replacement of joists damaged by dry rot or insects.

- Joists may need additional strength for new loads.

- Openings may be required in joists to accommodate piping or ducts.

Any joists damaged by moisture or dry rot should be replaced, after correcting the cause of the damage to ensure that it won't recur. The next step is to make sure the remodeled floor will support the intended loads. A special item to watch out for is the extra load imposed by a proposed **whirlpool** or **spa**. Always inform the builder, architect, or whoever is in charge of the structural integrity of the home that a spa is proposed and give them the weight of the unit, filled. For example, a spa containing 50 gallons (192L) of water and two people will weigh around 800 pounds (362kg), which must be distributed over a small area, amounting to around 60 psf (2.87 kN/m^2). Floors are usually designed for 40 psf (1.92 kN/m^2) loads, so joists under the immediate area should be at least doubled for any new load. The spa supplier should be able to give you this information and even suggest ways to reinforce the floor. A sister joist can be the same depth or shallower than the main joist but should extend to the supports, if possible. Joists can be beefed up by attaching (scabbing) a second "sister" joist onto the joists or by adding a pair of doubled new joists.

Figure 7.8 Existing wood floor framing can be strengthened by attaching sister joists. Ideally, the sister joists run full length to the bearing points.

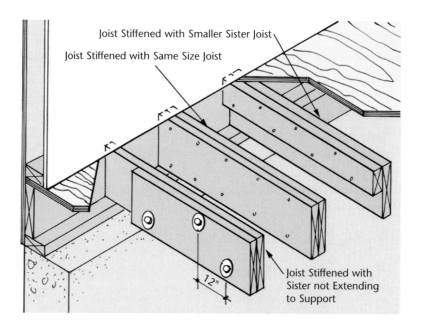

Framing floors to accommodate new plumbing will inevitably require cutting or notching the joists. Doing this without compromising the structural integrity of the joists requires planning. Typical requirements for fixtures include the following:

- Tub traps. Allow at least 4 inches (102 mm) clear from each side of the drain centerline and 12 inches (305 mm) from the wall to the drain.

- Shower drains. Allow an 8x8-inch (203 mm x 203 mm) space for the trap, centered below the drain and at least 3 inches (76 mm) additional clear space for access.

- Shower pans. Tiled shower floors typically require a recess in the framing to allow for mortar.

- Spas. Determine total weight of unit when full of water and provide framing adequate for the load. If the unit is to be set in mortar, add the weight of the mortar to the total.

Relocating plumbing fixtures during remodeling often entails re-routing the piping in the floor. Re-routing piping that runs below joists, as in a floor above an unfinished basement, can be done without affecting the floor structure. But some situations can jeopardize the structure. Joists have to be left largely intact to maintain their capacity to support the loads of the floor. Any cutting or notching of a joist must be done in a manner that leaves the joist with a safe carrying capacity.

For example, you may propose moving a toilet out into the room a few feet from its original location. While this looks fine in plan, it has serious implications for the joists below. The drain can run clear of any obstructions if the joists run parallel to it, but it will be too large to pass through a joist running perpendicular, regardless of its depth and species. Holes and notches in joists are limited both by their size and location in the joist. The IBC/2000 Code, section 2308.8.2 limits notching as follows:

Notches on the ends of joists shall not exceed one-fourth the joist depth. Holes bored in joists shall not be within 2 inches (51 mm) of the top or bottom of the joist, and the diameter of any such hole shall not exceed one-third the depth of the joist. Notches in the top or bottom of joists shall not exceed one-sixth the depth and shall not be located in the middle third of the span.

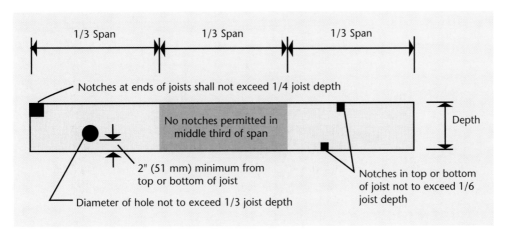

Figure 7.9 When holes or notches in joists are necessary to accommodate wiring or piping, care must be taken not to weaken their structural capacity.

Insulating a Wood Floor Above a Crawl Space

Kitchen and bath floors above crawl spaces should contain insulation to stem heat loss and a vapor barrier to keep moisture out. Insulation can go either between the floor joists or at the foundation wall. Insulating the floor itself allows the crawl space to be continuously ventilated (required by some local codes) but is harder to do. Also, any water pipes and heating ducts that run under or within the floor must be wrapped.

On the other hand, the foundation can be easily insulated on the inside or outside face. However, any vents in the wall must be closeable during the cold season. The location of the insulation also affects where the vapor-control barrier goes. If the floor joist cavities are insulated, the barrier should go between the insulation and room above, usually between the floor joists and subfloor. The best vapor barrier is a sheet of polyethylene at least 4 mils thick. The foil or Kraft paper facing on batt and blanket insulation is not a reliable vapor barrier. If you choose to insulate the foundation walls rather than the floor, the vapor barrier should go next to the inside face of the wall and extend completely over the soil below the crawl space.

Another way to insulate the foundation is to apply rigid foam to the outside of the crawl space, but this is more easily done on new construction. An existing foundation will have to first be excavated down to the footing.

Figure 7.10 An insulated floor over a cold basement/crawl space. All water supply piping and heating ducts must be fully insulated.

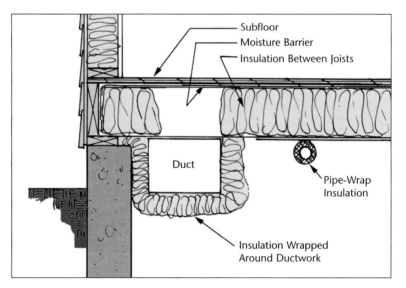

Subfloor

Moisture Barrier

Insulation Between Joists

Duct

Pipe-Wrap Insulation

Insulation Wrapped Around Ductwork

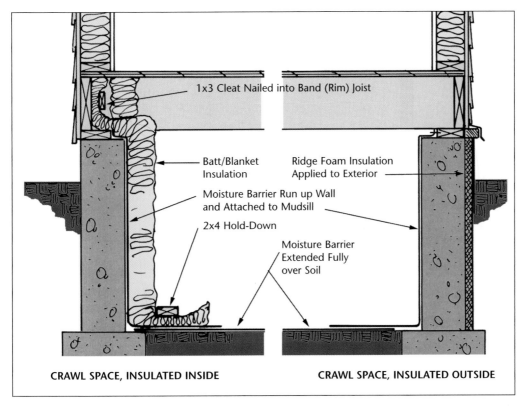

1x3 Cleat Nailed into Band (Rim) Joist

Batt/Blanket Insulation

Ridge Foam Insulation Applied to Exterior

Moisture Barrier Run up Wall and Attached to Mudsill

2x4 Hold-Down

Moisture Barrier Extended Fully over Soil

CRAWL SPACE, INSULATED INSIDE

CRAWL SPACE, INSULATED OUTSIDE

Figure 7.11 Foundations can be insulated on the inside (left) or outside (right). If the foundation is for a crawl space, as shown, a continuous vapor barrier is necessary down the wall and across the soil to keep soil moisture out of the interior.

Leveling Wood Floors

Wood-framed floors in old houses often slope from years of unequal settling. There are two main ways to level them:

- Removing the flooring and subfloor and scabbing sister joists to the existing joists, with the sisters placed at the desired level

- Applying a self-leveling compound over the surface.

Available in bags for jobsite mixing or installed by franchisers, leveling compounds consist of gypsum- or Portland cement-based mixes that are poured over almost any solid substrate, including wood and ceramic or vinyl tiles. You must first assess the condition of the framing to ensure it is strong enough to bear the additional load of the leveling compound. For example, adding 3/4 inch (19 mm) of a gypsum-based leveling compound can add around 7 psf (0.34 kN/m^2) to the floor. Rotted subfloor must first be replaced, preferably with 3/4-inch plywood. Loose subfloor must be screwed down firmly to the joists. Small holes must be filled and large holes covered with sheet metal or plywood. Cracks and edges must be sealed with drywall joint compound.

CONCRETE FLOORS

If concrete is the universal material for basement floors why can't it be used for above grade floors in homes with no basement? It can in many homes, especially in the south, where the danger of cracked concrete due to freezing is less. You may occasionally encounter structural concrete floor slabs in multi-story housing, but more often you will see it as "slab-on-grade" first floors of single homes. The typical slab-on-grade floor consists of a poured concrete slab over a layer of granular material such as sand or gravel, a vapor barrier and the earth. The granular layer distributes the load of the concrete evenly over the ground and allows any water below to drain without being trapped. The vapor barrier, usually a 4- or 6-mil-thick sheet of polyethylene plastic, prevents soil moisture from wicking up through the concrete.

Slab-on-grade floors make an excellent substrate for several finish materials and are well suited to radiant floor heating systems, where the tubing carrying hot water is imbedded in the slab. The slab distributes heat from the tubes evenly over the entire surface, without hot or cold spots. And because concrete is dense, it holds heat well, so it evens out the temperature swings over the course of a 24-hour period. Concrete floors are often seen in passive solar homes, where they are placed near south-facing windows to soak up solar heat during the day and release it at night, yielding comfort and lowering heating bills in the process.

The Downsides

Remember all those pipes, wires and ducts that snake through a typical basement ceiling or below a crawl space? Except for drainage piping, they all have to move somewhere else with a slab-on-grade floor. Heating ducts can be run below slabs, but this is expensive and inflexible, should any changes have to be made in the future. And if you have done much remodeling, you know that change is a given with most houses. Most of the piping will move upward, into the partitions and attic. Pipes should be insulated on the topside to prevent heat loss and gain (and prevent freezing, in the case of water pipes). You can run electrical wiring below slabs, but only encased in conduit and because it is now inaccessible to change, it usually makes better sense to run wiring in partitions or attics.

Cracking and differential settling are the main problems with concrete slabs themselves. Concrete shrinks when cooled and the shrinking can cause cracking. Reinforcing slabs with steel can help but not prevent shrinkage cracking.

The more reliable antidote is to make sure the concrete itself is of top quality. Start with the proper mix design (4,000 psi minimum strength) and specify a thick mix. The thicker the mix, the stronger the slab and the fewer the cracks. Specify a maximum slump of 4 inches. Fiberglass strands added to the mix boost its resistance to shrinkage and cracking. Specifications should also require the slab be poured under weather conditions not too hot or cold. After pouring and finishing, the slab should be covered and kept wet to allow it to develop full strength before drying out. In cold climates, a layer of rigid foam insulation under the slab not only helps avoid the temperature swings that can crack the slab but provides better comfort above.

Remodeling Concerns

Settling occurs in all slabs over time. It happens most often when the base material is not solid. Soils containing organic material (topsoils), clay and silt, are not suitable. Well-compacted gravel and sand make good substrates.

Slab-on-grade floors are constructed in two common configurations —"floating" within the concrete perimeter foundation or as an integral part of a shallow grade beam foundation. Floating slabs, if not tied to the foundation with reinforcing steel, can settle over time at the joint. When remodeling a bathroom in a house with such a slab, you might notice a gap between the wall and the floor baseboard. If the gap is significant, you might address the problem by stripping the finish from the slab and applying a floor-leveling compound before applying a new finish material.

Integral slab-on-grade/grade beam floors tend to crack out away from the edge. If the crack produces a change in level of the floor, it, too, might be leveled with leveling compound.

Figure 7.12 Slab-on-grade floors are vulnerable to cracking or settling at the perimeter. The settling in the slab shown (above) can be prevented with steel rebars doweled into the slab and foundation. The best preventative for cracks near the grade beam (below) is an adequate base material well compacted.

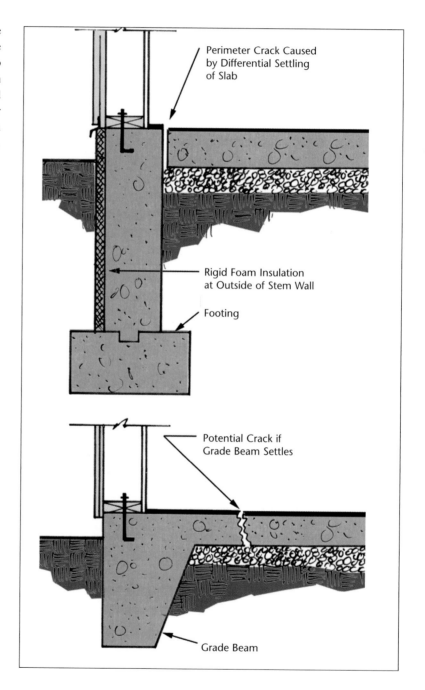

Perimeter Crack Caused by Differential Settling of Slab

Rigid Foam Insulation at Outside of Stem Wall

Footing

Potential Crack if Grade Beam Settles

Grade Beam

Because moisture passes easily through concrete, it is a constant danger to any floor finish placed on a slab. When designing a kitchen/bath in a remodeling project, look for curled seams or bubbles under sheet flooring. Specify that all existing flooring be completely removed, along with the adhesive, before new flooring is applied.

Another concern is the piping and heating ducts that may underlie a slab in a slab-on-grade home. Re-routing these lines may entail removing a portion of the slab, which can be costly.

Old slabs may have settled unevenly, putting them out-of-level. They can be put right with self-leveling compound, as described above for out-of-level wood floors.

SUBFLOORS AND UNDERLAYMENTS

A quality floor finish starts with what lies beneath. Concrete slabs, if dry and smooth can serve well as the substrate for ceramic tile, sheet flooring or carpeting. Selecting the right substrate for framed floors is more complicated than for a concrete slab because the substrate may consist of multiple layers. If the subfloor does double duty as a platform plus underlayment, its surface must suit the intended floorcovering. Some plywood products are made with this in mind.

Subfloor Materials

When specifying a substrate for a wood- or steel-framed floor, consider first the strength requirements of the subfloor. It must be stiff enough to span between the joists, so make sure the material is rated for the actual joist spacing to be used. Plywood and oriented strand board (OSB) are the two most common subfloor materials in use today. Use the span rating number on the panel to match the material and thickness to the joist spacing. Here are some of the most common subfloor materials.

Plywood. The most universal underlayment, plywood is available in a species and grade suited to every floorcovering. All American Plywood Association (APA) approved underlayments are classified as "Exposure 1" or "Exterior." Exposure 1 resists limited exposure to weather during construction, but is not as dependable against long-term moisture as Exterior, which is a better choice for bathroom floors. B or C face veneers are suitable for ceramic tile. Resilient flooring requires a smooth, fully sanded face. PTS plywood is sanded only in spots, hence is not as desirable as plywood stamped "Sanded Face."

Oriented strand board. Oriented strand board (OSB) consists of long, narrow wood chips produced by slicing the wood across the grain. The strands are oriented in cross directions, with the outer layers running essentially parallel to the length of the panel, similar to plywood and about as stiff. Heat and phenolic resin bonds the strands together. OSB subflooring comes in 4x8-foot (1,219 mm x 2,438 mm) sheets with tongue-and-groove joints. The most common thickness is 3/4 inch (19 mm). Like plywood, OSB bears grade stamps that indicate its quality and uses.

Underlayments

Plywood. Fir and pine plywood used for the subfloor may also serve as an underlayment if the surface grade meets the requirements of the floorcovering.

Luan plywood. A type of mahogany available in 1/4-inch (6 mm) thickness, has met with increasing acceptance for resilient flooring. It carries two ratings from the International Hardwood Products Association. Type 1 has exterior glue. Type 2 has water-resistant glue. Only Type 1 should be used for underlayment under resilient floorcovering (look for the grade on the edge, rather than the face, of the panel).

Particleboard. The perfectly smooth, knot free and impact-resistant surface of particleboard make it highly desirable for an underlayment for carpet. But its tendency to absorb moisture, particularly at the edges, makes it unsuitable for resilient floorcovering, ceramic tile and stone.

Hardboard. Like particleboard, hardboard's surface is smooth and consistent. It remains a popular underlayment material despite newer materials, but resilient flooring manufacturers differ in their acceptance of it for resilient tiles or sheet goods. The Resilient Floor Covering Institute (RFCI) recommends it as one of two acceptable underlayments for resilient flooring, the other being plywood of the appropriate grade. However the recommendation applies only to Class 4 service-grade hardboard, 0.215 inches (5 mm) thick, which is scarce. Some resilient flooring manufacturers do not allow hardboard for fully adhered floorcoverings because of its alleged poor uniformity, dimensional instability and variable surface porosity. The tightly packed fibers also make it unsuited to moist environments. So while it may work for a kitchen floor, it's a poor choice in a bathroom.

Cement Board. An excellent underlayment for ceramic tile floors, other than inside showers, is made of Portland cement reinforced with thin wire mesh, called **cement board** or **cement backerboard**. Cement board panels, 24 by 48 inches by 1/2-inch thick (610 mm x 1,219 mm x 13 mm), are screwed or nailed to the subfloor. After the joints are taped with fiberglass-mesh joint tape using drywall compound, the substrate is ready for ceramic tile.

Self-Leveling Compounds. If a self-leveling compound is used to even out a sloping floor (as described on page 69 under "Leveling Wood Floors) the compound also provides a suitable substrate for most floorcoverings.

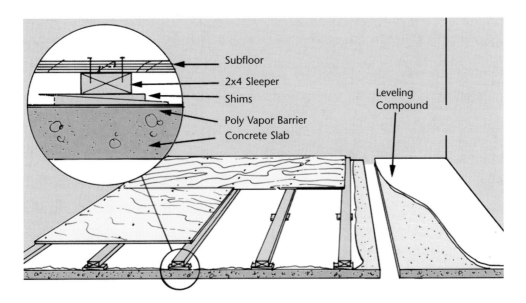

Subfloor
2x4 Sleeper
Shims
Poly Vapor Barrier
Concrete Slab
Leveling Compound

Figure 7.13 Concrete floors are leveled with wood sleepers, shimmed (left side of drawing), or by leveling compound poured over the surface (right). Sleepers offer other benefits, such as cavities for running wiring or placing insulation, and a means of attaching wood flooring.

Matching the Substrate to the Floor Finish			
Finish Material	**Supporting Structure**	**Subfloor**	**Underlayment**
Ceramic tile Quarry tile Stone tile	Wood/steel joists	Plywood OSB	Cement board
	Concrete slab	(The slab)	None for thinsetting Mortar bed for mudsetting
	Concrete slab plus wood sleepers	Plywood OSB	Cement board
Resilient sheet flooring or tiles	Wood/steel joists	Plywood	(None if plywood smooth) 1/4-inch plywood, otherwise
		OSB	1/4-inch plywood
	Concrete slab	(The slab, smoothed)	(The slab, smoothed)
	Concrete slab plus wood sleepers	Plywood	(None if plywood smooth) 1/4-inch plywood, otherwise
		OSB	1/4-inch plywood
Wood strips or planks (traditional)	Wood/steel joists	Plywood OSB	(None)
	Concrete slab plus wood sleepers	Plywood OSB	(None)
Glue-down parquets, planks, strips	Wood/steel joists	Plywood	(None, if plywood smooth) 1/4-inch plywood, otherwise
		OSB	1/4-inch plywood
	Concrete slab Concrete slab plus wood sleepers	(The slab, smoothed) Plywood	(The slab, smoothed) (None if plywood smooth) 1/4-inch plywood, otherwise
		OSB	1/4-inch plywood
Edge-glued floating veneer flooring	Wood/steel joists	Plywood OSB	(None)
	Concrete slab	(The slab, smoothed)	1/8-inch-thick closed-cell foam padding
	Concrete slab plus wood sleepers	Plywood OSB	

CASE STUDY #1 –
NEW BATH FIXTURES ON A CONCRETE FLOOR

The owners of a summer home on a New Hampshire lake wanted to finish part of their basement to accommodate visiting guests. The basement had enough space for a new bedroom and a niche that contained a washer and dryer seemed the best location for a bath if water supply and waste lines could be installed without incurring too much cost. The main obstacle was the concrete slab-on-grade floor. The solution to the problem was to locate a small three-fixture bath in the unused portion of the laundry niche. Hot- and cold-water piping was run in the ceiling, then down the back wall to serve the new fixtures. A waste line was extended off the existing floor drain by saw-cutting a 6-foot-long strip of the concrete slab. The slab was then patched and tiled to create a finished floor surface.

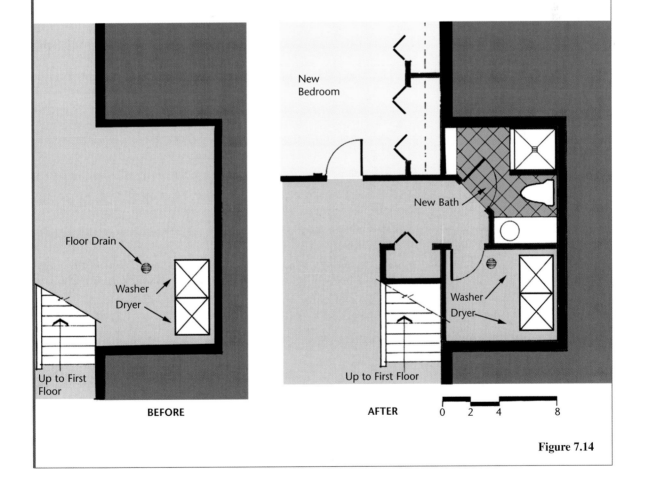

BEFORE

AFTER

Figure 7.14

CHAPTER 8: Exterior Walls

This book began by asking you to think of a house as a collection of systems. In the last chapter we saw how floor systems are constructed to meet specific criteria. Exterior walls comprise another important house system. Their tasks are several: keep the weather out, provide privacy, support fixtures and cabinetry, to name a few. Some outside walls also support parts of the house. In this chapter we'll see how various wall systems meet these challenges.

FRAMING SYSTEMS

Framed walls take several forms. Most of your kitchen and bath work will probably focus on homes built of lightweight structural systems, but other systems are also in use, so you should be prepared to deal with them

Log Homes

Trees covered the Eastern coast of North America when the first settlers set foot on its soil. Not surprisingly, they used this most readily available material to build their homes. Even unskilled homeowners could put up a shelter quickly by stacking logs on each other horizontally. The only part requiring any carpentry skills were the corners, which had to be notched to interlock. The gaps between logs were chinked (packed) with mud or, if available, mortar, to seal out the drafts. Nostalgia among some homeowners to return this rustic simplicity has spurred a resurgence of log homes in recent decades. Today specialty manufacturers supply the log homes as kits of pre-shaped logs, cut to length and erected by franchised contractors.

Cedar makes up most of today's log homes. Left exposed on the outside, it may or may not be exposed on the inside, depending on the interior finish and insulation requirements. And insulation is the Achilles' heel of log home construction. Wood is inherently a poor insulator. To bring a log wall up to an R-19 level as required by most energy codes, the logs must be around 19 inches (483 mm) thick. Since the standard thickness of log home logs is 6 inches, additional insulation must be added. Some systems do this by fitting pieces of rigid foam in slots cut into the logs. Others simply rely on insulation added inside, which conceals the logs. Manufacturers have, however, been more successful at controlling infiltration by creatively using gaskets and other types of seals between logs.

Plumbing can't be run through log walls, so any pipes for kitchen and bath walls must be located inside the exterior walls and concealed behind a finish material.

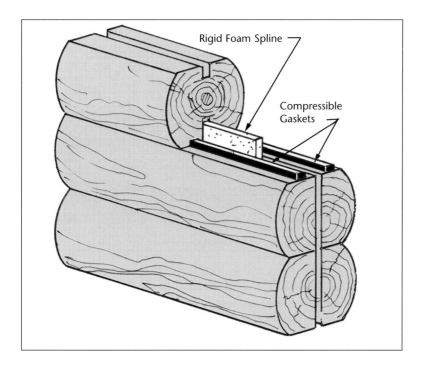

Rigid Foam Spline

Compressible Gaskets

Figure 8.1 One log home system sandwiches rigid foam strips into grooves in the logs and uses compressible gaskets to make an air seal between the logs.

Post-and-Beam Framing

Another wall framing system that has gained ground in recent years also has its roots in colonial times. In post-and-beam framing (also called timber framing), beams support floors and roofs and transferred their loads to vertical posts, which take them to the foundation. Structural joints shaped with mortise and tenon joints fit precisely, with nothing more than wood pegs to connect the parts. The infill wall portions between the posts have only to keep the weather outside.

Today several specialty manufacturers (timber framers) scattered around the U.S. design timber framing systems, sometimes collaborating with architects or home designers. After cutting and shaping the parts, they ship them to the site and either erect them or engage a knowledgeable local contractor for this task. Infill wall panels are either standard studwall construction or structural-insulated panels (SIPs), which are sandwiches of rigid foam insulation cores faced with OSB or plywood. SIPs go up quickly and make very tight, well-insulated envelopes for post-and-beam houses.

Figure 8.2 A typical post-and-beam framing system. SIP panels attached to the outside provide insulation and closure, allowing the framing members to be exposed inside.

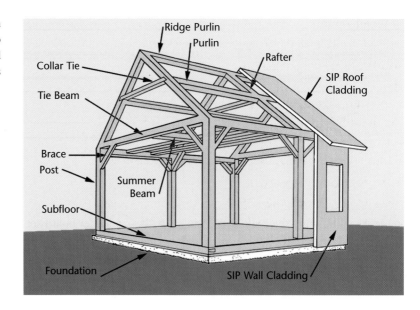

Figure 8.3 SIP panels are gaining ground as an alternative to site-built studwalls. The panels sandwich rigid foam insulation between sheets of OSB, with 2x4s on the perimeters.

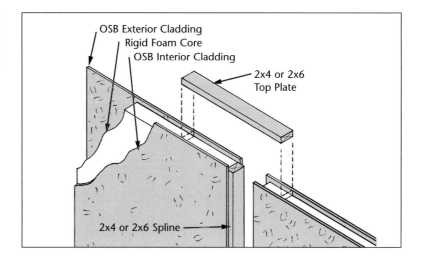

Studwall Framing

The advent of wire nails combined with improved sawmill technology in the first half of the nineteenth century revolutionized housing construction. Instead of a few heavy wood members that could only be joined by skilled craftsmen, houses could be constructed entirely of assemblies of light members and the whole structure held together by nails. The roofs of single-story houses could now bear directly on a plate supported by regularly spaced studs.

For the two-story house, two systems emerged. In the first, **balloon framing**, studs extend from mudsill to eaves. The first floor joists bear on the mudsill, while the second floor joists bear on a ledger board set in notches in the studs. But the system had one major downside: the joist spacing had to match the stud spacing exactly. Because of this, balloon framing gave way to a simpler system, **platform framing**. Studs in platform-framed walls span between the floors, or platforms. The first floor studs bear on a band joist and extend to the bottom of the band joist of the second floor. Second floor joists extend from this to the roof plate. Because of its simpler and speedier construction, platform framing is the method of choice today. When working with balloon framing, you may be required by code to place fire blocks between the studs.

Figure 8.4 Balloon framing, encountered in some old houses, stretches wall studs from mudsill to roof. Second floor joists bear on a ledger notched into the studs. Floor joists must be planned to align perfectly with the studs.

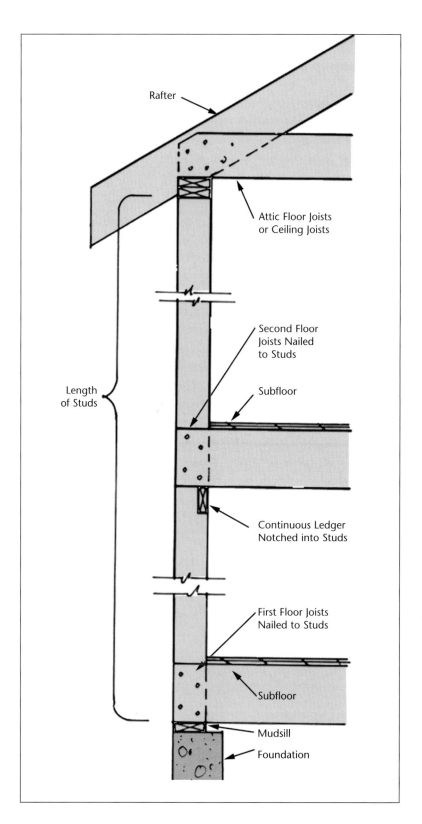

Rafter

Attic Floor Joists or Ceiling Joists

Length of Studs

Second Floor Joists Nailed to Studs

Subfloor

Continuous Ledger Notched into Studs

First Floor Joists Nailed to Studs

Subfloor

Mudsill

Foundation

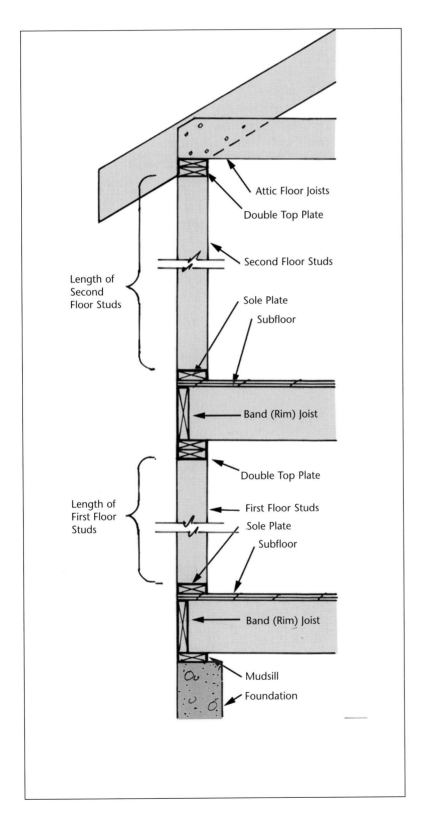

Figure 8.5 Today's houses use platform framing because of its simpler construction. After the first floor wall is erected, the second floor, or platform, goes on, followed by the walls of the next floor.

If the wall is a bearing wall, the studs carry any vertical loads from the roof and floors down to the foundation. Studwalls must also be braced to resist horizontal wind and seismic forces. Bracing in the earliest studwalls consisted of boards on an angle notched into the studs at the corners. Plywood or OSB panels have replaced angle bracing in most present-day homes. Local codes define horizontal bracing requirements, as well as other provisions necessary to make the structure resistant to high winds or earthquake danger prevalent in the region.

Each stud of a load-bearing wall shares part of the vertical load from above. 2x4s spaced 16 inches (406 mm) apart ("on center" or "o.c."), the standard of the past, has been replaced in cold-climate areas with 2x6s, to accommodate the thicker insulation of today's energy codes. When 2x6s are used, their spacing is often increased to 24 inches, in the interest of economy, but any cost saved on lumber has to be traded off against heavier interior wall cladding. If gypsum drywall is used, 1/2-inch-thick (13 mm) panels should be increased to 5/8-inch thick (16 mm) to be stiff enough.

Figure 8.6 A typical exterior studwall contains double studs at the top plate, corners, and openings. Headers above the openings are sized to support the loads imposed above. Corner bracing is required to resist seismic and lateral forces. Bracing may consist of OSB or plywood panels or metal tees.

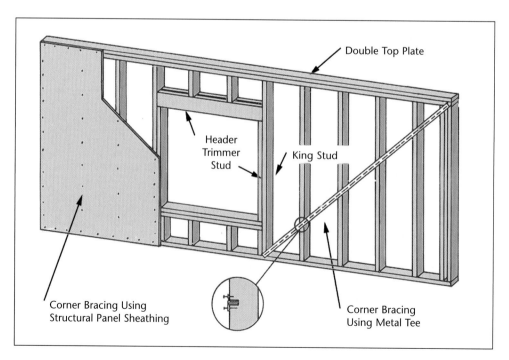

Double Top Plate

Header
Trimmer
Stud

King Stud

Corner Bracing Using
Structural Panel Sheathing

Corner Bracing
Using Metal Tee

Lightweight Steel Wall Framing

In the last chapter we saw how light-gauge steel joists are making steady inroads into the construction of floors in houses. There are corresponding wall-framing members consisting of C-shaped studs and stud runners. The framing goes up quickly, held together with sheet metal screws. But steel stud wall framing faces the same obstacles in home building as was mentioned for steel-framed floors: unfamiliar technique for carpenters, special tools and equipment. And there is one other problem with steel-framed exterior walls. Steel's excellent ability to conduct heat makes an easy path for heat to escape to the outside, bypassing the cavity insulation. Any moisture that finds its way into the wall condenses on the cold outer flange of the stud where it rots the sheathing. Homebuilders have gotten around this problem by either applying rigid foam insulation to the outside faces of the studs or avoiding steel stud framing entirely on exterior walls.

Wall Sheathing

If you think of studs as the bones of a wood- or steel-framed home, the sheathing constitutes the skin. Wall sheathing is the membrane material that clads the outer face of the studs, tying them together into a single structural system and providing an anchor for finish materials. Pine boards were the sheathing of choice for homes built prior to the 1940s. Installed diagonally, they formed triangles, which braced the studs against horizontal forces. The plywood that eventually eased out board sheathing is itself being edged out by cheaper OSB panels.

Insulating Framed Walls

In Chapter 4 we learned that the insulation system of a home consists of two parts: thermal insulation and an air/vapor barrier. Thermal insulation can be installed at four possible locations in framed walls:

- On the outer face of the sheathing

- At the inside face of the studs (sandwiched between the studs and wall finish)

- In the cavities between the studs

- Some combination of the above

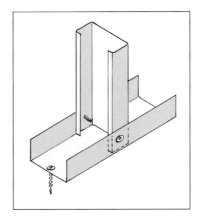

Figure 8.7 Lightweight steel studs are seeing increasing use for wall framing in homes. The system consists of C-shaped studs that fit into C-shaped runners, attached with sheet metal screws.

Because vapor barriers are so important to high-moisture areas, such as kitchens and baths, they must be installed in the correct position with respect to the insulation to work. Here's how you might correctly specify an insulating/vapor barrier system in a new wall:

1. Determine the desired R-value. (See Chapter 4.)

2. Determine whether the vapor barrier will go inside or outside the insulation (by whether the region is dominated by the need for heating or cooling).

3. Compare the costs for achieving the desired R-value and vapor barrier with various types of insulation available in your area.

The last item is the hardest, since it involves tradeoffs with other materials. If you want an R-19 wall, for example, you will need insulation with a total R-value of R-18 (you get a credit of about R-1 for the inside and outside air film). Filling the cavities between 2x4 studs with standard R-11 fiberglass insulation yields R-12 (or R-16, with high-density fiberglass). You can increase this to the desired level by adding an inch of rigid polyurethane insulation to the inside (R-7.2 per inch), or by using 2x6 studs and R-19 fiberglass.

The differential cost of wider studs must be compared to the costs of the insulation. But fiberglass used alone requires a separate vapor barrier, usually a sheet of 4- or 6-mil poly sheet stapled to the inside of the wall after the insulation is in place. You can avoid a separate vapor barrier with a hybrid approach combining foil-faced rigid foam with fiberglass cavity insulation. The foil facing is an excellent moisture barrier, but the system works only if the joints are taped.

Figure 8.8 2x4 studs with R-10 insulation between no longer meet the energy codes of many states. One alternative is to use 2x6 studs with R-19 insulation (left). Another uses 2x6 studs with R-10 between and an additional layer of rigid foam (right) on the inside to increase the total R-value to the required level. This system yields the additional advantage of obtaining an easy vapor barrier by taping the joints of the rigid foam.

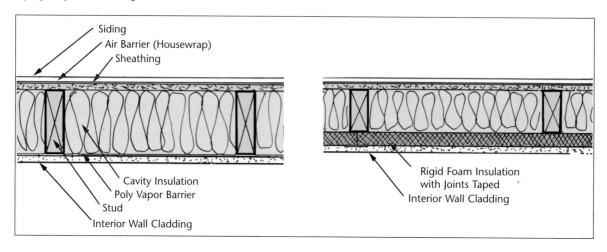

Siding
Air Barrier (Housewrap)
Sheathing

Cavity Insulation
Poly Vapor Barrier
Stud
Interior Wall Cladding

Rigid Foam Insulation
with Joints Taped
Interior Wall Cladding

Insulating Existing Walls

The exterior walls of old houses are often under-insulated or totally uninsulated. People like their baths to be cozy and warm, which requires well-insulated walls. And because baths generate a lot of moisture, the walls should also contain adequate barriers to moisture passage. For these reasons it is not in the owner's interest to undertake extensive improvements to the interior without making sure the exterior walls are up to par. Before planning an upgrade, investigate the existing walls to see how they are put together. You might get an idea by simply removing a cover plate of a switch or outlet in an outside wall. If not, a test hole might be necessary.

There are three basic approaches to adding insulation to existing framed walls:

- Blow loose-fill insulation into the cavities from the outside or inside.

- Strip off the interior surface and insulate the cavities.

- Add insulation onto the inside surface.

Whichever method you choose, make sure the system includes a moisture barrier.

Blown Insulation. Cellulose and fiberglass loose-fill insulation are blown into the walls through holes cut in either the outside or inside finish/sheathing layers. If applied from the outside, the insulation contractor removes siding boards at intervals along the outer wall, drills holes in the sheathing between each stud and inserts a hose to fill the cavity. After replacing the siding, the original appearance of the exterior of the home is restored with no trace of the work. For inside jobs, holes are cut in the interior surface and patched after the cavities are filled. The downside to either method, especially in baths, is the lack of a moisture barrier. If a new interior finish is planned, a layer of poly can be installed beneath the finish to provide one.

Figure 8.9 One way to insulate an existing frame home is to remove siding at intervals, drill holes in the sheathing and blow loose fiber insulation into the cavities. The holes are then patched and the siding replaced.

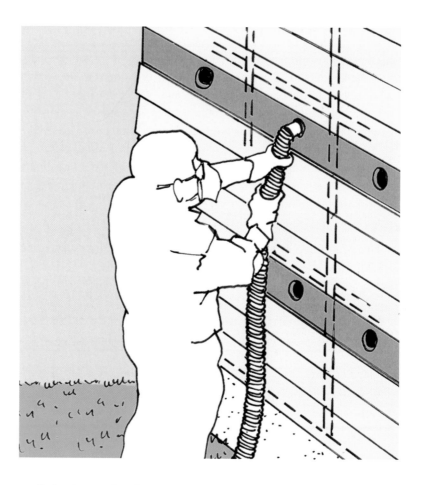

Stripping and Filling. If the inside surface must be replaced for other reasons or removed to access the cavities for wiring or plumbing work, the easiest way to insulate the wall cavities is to install any of the types of cavity insulation described previously before applying a moisture barrier and new interior surface.

Adding Insulation Onto the Interior. The easiest, most economical method might be to leave the existing wall alone and add an insulated layer onto the inside surface. If the room is large enough to spare the space, erect a studwall inside the outside wall. The cavities can contain any new piping and wiring, as well as the insulation. If space is too small for a new studwall, rigid foam insulation can be applied to the surface of the existing interior finish, set between strapping applied horizontally to the wall at 24-inch (610 mm) intervals. The strapping provides a base for attachment of the new wall substrate and finish materials. Moisture control is by either applying a poly vapor barrier over the foam/strapping or by taping all of the joints (but only with foil-faced insulation).

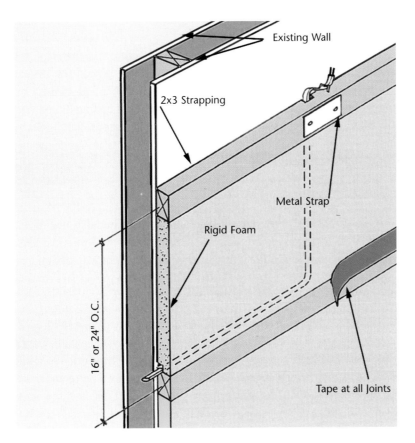

Existing Wall

2x3 Strapping

Metal Strap

Rigid Foam

16" or 24" O.C.

Tape at all Joints

Figure 8.10 Wood strips (strapping) attached to the inside face of an existing wall provides a way to both add insulation and wiring to the wall, without removing the wall's surface. Metal straps are required where cables penetrate the strapping to protect the cables from puncture by nails.

MASONRY WALLS

Masonry is the art of assembling stone, brick and other heavy mineral-based materials with or without mortar. All masonry materials are massive, high in compressive strength and immune to decay from organic sources—good properties for a homebuilding material. But masonry materials are also porous, which allows moisture to pass through. While they retain heat well—a useful property in passive solar homes—they are poor insulators, necessitating insulation in exterior masonry walls. Finally, while masonry has high compressive strength, it requires steel reinforcement to make up for its lack of tensile strength. That said, the widespread use of masonry materials in homebuilding makes them worthy of your comprehension.

Concrete

While not strictly a masonry material, concrete has many of the same characteristics. The material consists of small-size stone (aggregate), sand and Portland cement, catalyzed into a solid form by the addition of water. In use for years for residential foundation and floor slabs, concrete is now seeing use in above-grade walls, thanks to new forming systems that use foam plastic to form the concrete, as discussed in Chapter 7.

Concrete Block

Often seen in foundations, concrete blocks are also the basic material of above-grade walls in some homes, especially in southern regions. Their susceptibility to cracking makes them less popular in colder regions. Concrete made with small-diameter gravel and sand is used to pre-cast concrete masonry units (CMUs), or concrete blocks.

Blocks come in several modular shapes and sizes, each tailored to a specific use. The most common thickness for walls up to 8 feet (2,438 mm) high is nominally 8 inches (actually 7 5/8 inches, or 194 mm). Blocks can be set in mortar or dry-set, by simply laying them up without mortar, then troweling a pre-packaged surface-bonding mix over each face. Both setting methods require steel to reinforce the walls both horizontally and vertically. Like concrete walls, block walls are poor insulators in themselves. Above-grade walls can be insulated on either face or by using a special type of block that contains foam inserts. Interior surfaces can be left exposed, painted, or furred out to receive another wall finish.

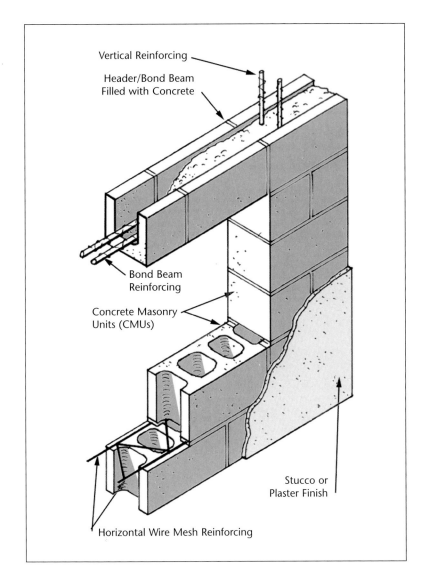

Vertical Reinforcing

Header/Bond Beam
Filled with Concrete

Bond Beam
Reinforcing

Concrete Masonry
Units (CMUs)

Stucco or
Plaster Finish

Horizontal Wire Mesh Reinforcing

Figure 8.11 A typical concrete block (CMU) wall. Reinforcing is determined by the engineering requirements and local codes. The wall contains wire mesh (ladder) reinforcement at every 6th course, vertical rebars in grouted cores around openings and, where required by code, reinforced bond beams above openings and along the top of the wall.

Brick and Stone

Brick, a manufactured material, and stone, a natural one, are both favorite cladding. Because they are not considered as structural materials, they require a separate structural wall to support the floors and roofs of a house, as well as to provide horizontal backup for the masonry itself. The resulting double-wall assembly is thus called a masonry **veneer**. The most common masonry veneer walls in houses consist of wood or steel studs faced with brick or stone. In addition to providing lateral support for the masonry, the studs also provide cavities for insulation, wiring and pipes and a substrate for attaching interior finishes.

Figure 8.12 Brick veneer walls rely on studs or masonry backups for structural support. An air space between the two wall layers and proper flashing are required to prevent water from penetrating the inner wall.

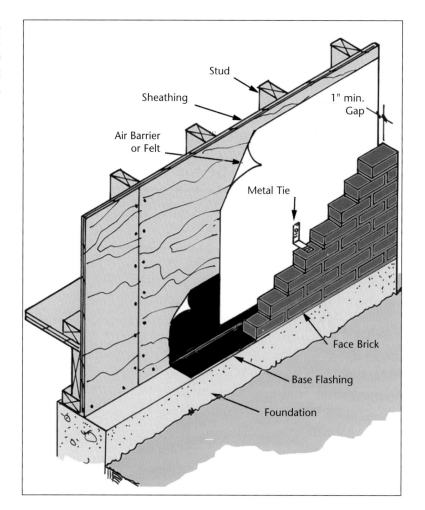

EXTERIOR FINISHES

Walls other than brick or stone require an applied finish material capable of withstanding the elements and consistent with the style of the home and regional requirements. The choices are numerous, both in material composition, sizes and shapes. About the only thing they have in common is that most are installed by nailing to a substrate of rigid sheathing. Here are some of the most common residential cladding materials.

Wood Board Siding

Real wood siding is the cladding of choice for many homeowners willing to maintain it. Wood is an organic material that changes over time by the effects of weather. Rot-resistant species such as redwood, cedar and cypress can be left uncoated. Near the seacoast, where it is continually subjected to moisture, wood siding weathers evenly to a uniform gray. To remain uniform in color in drier regions, the siding requires periodic application of a preservative, stain, or paint. Decay-prone species such as pine or spruce must be coated in any case.

If you want the very best, longest lasting wood siding for your clients, specify clear western red cedar or redwood pre-primed on all sides. The best quality comes from the heartwood of old-growth redwood or cedar trees. But their increasing scarcity has made this source too expensive for many homeowners, who must make do with a lesser grade of redwood or cedar containing knots or another species such as pine or spruce.

Wood siding comes in various profiles intended for horizontal or vertical installation. **Horizontal siding** boards overlap each other, attached to the wall by nails into the studs. **Vertical siding** is available in boards with rabbeted edges that overlap each other and as plain boards with smaller strips (battens) that cover the joints. The vertical joints of both configurations are prone to water penetration. For that reason, a good backup layer of felt (asphalt-impregnated building paper, tar paper) is first applied to the sheathing. The boards are then nailed to the wall at three points—top plate, mid-point blocking and bottom plate.

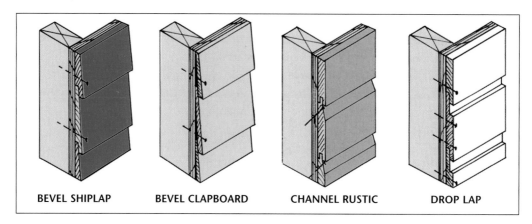

BEVEL SHIPLAP   **BEVEL CLAPBOARD**   **CHANNEL RUSTIC**   **DROP LAP**

Figure 8.13 All types of horizontal board siding attach to the wall with nails that penetrate the studs. The optimum location of the nails varies from one profile to the next.

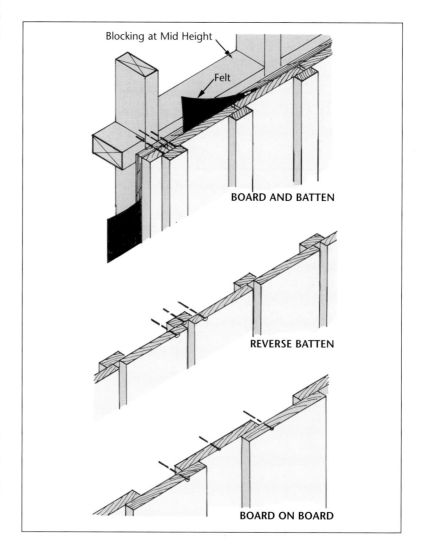

Blocking at Mid Height

Felt

BOARD AND BATTEN

REVERSE BATTEN

Figure 8.14 Vertical board siding is applied to a sheathed studwall over a layer of felt. Boards are nailed to the top and sill plates and blocking placed between studs at mid height.

BOARD ON BOARD

Shingles and Shakes

Cape Cod and some other traditional residential styles are unthinkable without their trademark siding of gray cedar **shingles**. Quality and price is highest for #1 red cedar shingles. Other species and prices are available, all in random widths 16 or 18 inches (406 or 457 mm) long, tapering from a point to about 1/2 inch (13 mm) at the butt end. Shingles install in overlapping layers over a weather barrier of asphalt-saturated building felt. The exposures, or "to weather" vertical dimensions, are usually 4 1/2 or 5 inches (114 or 127 mm). Each shingle is nailed independently, unless panelized shingles are used. Available in strips of 8 feet (2,438 mm) long, these cost more but go up much faster, saving on labor. Wood **shakes** offer a more rustic appearance. Split, rather than sawn from logs, shakes are thicker and more irregularly shaped. The exposed side is rough; the underside smooth.

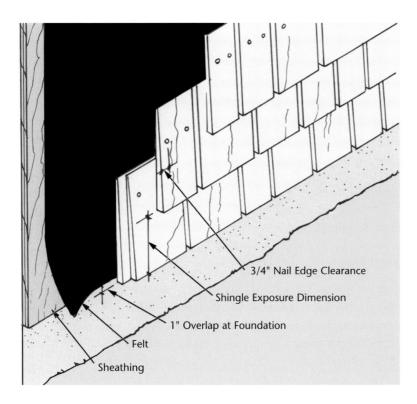

3/4" Nail Edge Clearance

Shingle Exposure Dimension

1" Overlap at Foundation

Felt

Sheathing

Figure 8.15 Shingle siding is nailed to a sheathed studwall over a layer of felt. Two nails attach each shingle close enough to the top to be concealed by the next course.

Composition Siding

A number of horizontal siding products made from wood composites are available as more economical alternatives to real wood. Some are made from wood chips or fibers bonded under heat and pressure with chemical resins. Others use wood fibers bonded together with Portland cement. The surface of either type can be smooth or embossed to resemble rough cedar. The boards come in 16-foot (4,877 mm) lengths of uniform consistency with no knots. **Cement-based siding** must be primed and painted on site. Wood composition siding comes pre-primed, to receive one or two finish coats after installation. **Wood composition siding** has recently come under fire for deteriorating under exposure to moisture, a particular concern in humid regions, so make sure any material you specify has a good track record for the intended location and is covered by a good warranty.

Plywood Panel Siding

Plywood siding is manufactured in panels of 4 feet by 8 feet (1,219 mm x 2,438 mm), 3/8-inch or 5/8-inch (10 mm or 16 mm) thick. Grooves cut part way through the surface create the impression of vertical boards spaced at 4 or 8 inches (102 mm or 203 mm). Plywood siding makes a good material for horizontal soffits. When installed as siding, the panels are positioned vertically over felt and nailed at three points, as with vertical board siding. The rabbeted vertical edges overlap each other. If the wall height exceeds the length of a single panel, the horizontal joints between the butt ends of successive panels must be flashed to prevent leaks. Redwood- and cedar-faced plywood siding can be painted, stained, or left unfinished. Fir- or pine-faced panels must be painted or stained.

Vinyl Siding

Low price (compared to quality wood siding) and easy maintenance has steadily increased the market share of vinyl siding for new houses as well as a replacement for deteriorated wood siding on existing houses. Vinyl siding is extruded from polyvinyl chloride (PVC) plastic in thin profiles and embossed to look like wood. Viewed up close, it is obviously not wood and the dead give away is the joints where the siding meets the trim. Because plastic expands and contracts significantly along its length, each siding length must run behind a vertical trim piece to allow it to move. The necessary gap between the trim and siding always differentiates vinyl siding from real wood siding that simply butts into the trim. Its appeal comes from the fact that, unlike wood, it never needs repainting. However, the durability of vinyl, over time, depends on the thickness of the material and the quality of the installation. A quality job starts with siding at least .044 inches thick. Lighter colors fare better than dark ones, which may fade in time.

Metal Siding

Aluminum and steel siding are stronger than vinyl and have other advantages. The pre-finished coatings hold dark colors better than vinyl and metal siding expands much less than plastic, making the trim more pleasing. Steel, the most expensive, is also the strongest. However the extra strength might prove worth the money in areas prone to high winds such as the Gulf South and Midwest.

Stucco and EIFS

Stucco is a traditional cladding that blends well with adjacent materials and can be applied both to framed and masonry walls. Composed of cement, lime and sand, stucco is troweled onto wire mesh reinforcing over a layer of building felt in three coats. The surface can be left uncoated or painted. To shed water dependably, joints with abutting trim and materials must be properly flashed and caulked.

Cold temperatures cause cementitious stucco to shrink and crack— its major flaw. A variety of synthetic exterior coatings grouped under the acronym "**EIFS**" (exterior insulation and finish systems) are elastic rather than rigid. They don't crack with temperature changes. EIFS use acrylic polymers as the binding material, alone, or combined with Portland cement. Developed as a low-cost alternative to stucco for commercial building facades, EIFS are appearing on an increasing number of homes. EIFS are applied in several layers over rigid foam insulation or directly onto a plywood or cement board substrate. Many textures and colors are available. The colorant is imbedded in the material, making it permanent and maintenance free. For all their advantages, EIFS have leaked in some homes, especially in the South. Manufacturers have responded by publishing installation details that allow any entrapped water to escape to the outside.

Figure 8.16 Exterior insulated finish and sheathing systems (EIFS) employ several layers—felt, rigid foam, fiberglass mesh, and two coats of elastomeric coating—to yield an insulated stucco-like finish. Proper detailing is required to prevent entrapped moisture.

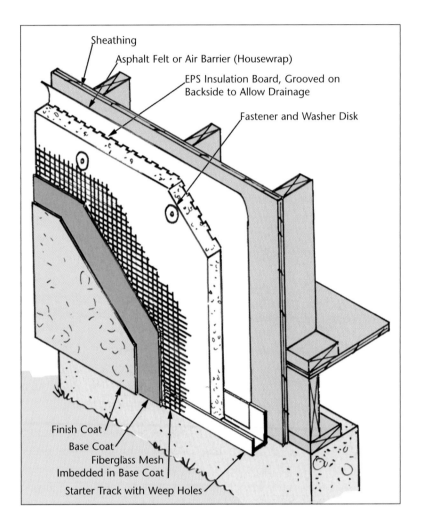

Sheathing

Asphalt Felt or Air Barrier (Housewrap)

EPS Insulation Board, Grooved on Backside to Allow Drainage

Fastener and Washer Disk

Finish Coat

Base Coat

Fiberglass Mesh Imbedded in Base Coat

Starter Track with Weep Holes

Siding Compared				
Siding	**Cost**	**Finishes**	**Pros**	**Cons**
Wood boards	High	Uncoated, Paint or stain	Attractive, durable	Periodic refinishing, can weather unevenly
OSB	Low	Pre-primed for top coat or pre-finished	Uniform lengths, knot free, stiffer than hardboard	Periodic refinishing, limited textures available
Hard-board	Low	Pre-primed for top coat or pre-finished	Uniform lengths, knot free, wide range of textures and patterns	Periodic refinishing
Plywood Panel	Low to medium	Paint or stain, cedar and redwood can remain unfinished	Fast installation	Limited patterns, needs flashing at butt ends
Vinyl	Low	No finish needed	Fast installation, no finish, long warranty	Vulnerable to impact damage, poor appearance at joints
Aluminum	High	Pre-finished	Durable, needs no finish	Dents under impact
Steel	High	Pre-finished	Durable, needs no finish, resists impact better than aluminum	
Shingles	High	Leave unfinished or stain	Good appearance, durable, choice of exposure widths	Weathers unevenly if unfinished, slow to install
Stucco	Medium	Uncoated, Paint or stain	Durable, long lasting	Prone to cracking and leaks
EIFS	High	Pre-finished	Looks like stucco, needs no finish, long-lasting, combines finish with insulation	Needs good detailing and meticulous installation to avoid water problems

EXTERIOR TRIMWORK

The right type of trimwork for the outside is just as important to a quality job as selecting the right siding. Good detailing at corners, roof edges, windows and doors not only affect appearance, but also are crucial to shedding water. The cladding material and style of the house together suggest the appropriate trim material and how it should be installed. Vinyl and metal siding are often trimmed with shapes of the same material. Quality wood siding deserves top grade wood or composite trim. Brick and stone also need wood trim for the eaves, windows and doors.

Corner Details

The inside and outside corners of wood and shingle siding can come together in several ways. Outside corners can be mitered (or woven, with shingles), covered with a metal trim piece, or abut a vertical trim board. Inside corners can meet a vertical inside trim board (all types) or be mitered or woven (shingles and shakes). Vertical trim boards typically go up before the siding. Vinyl, aluminum and steel siding usually terminate in trim of the same material, shaped to turn corners and angles.

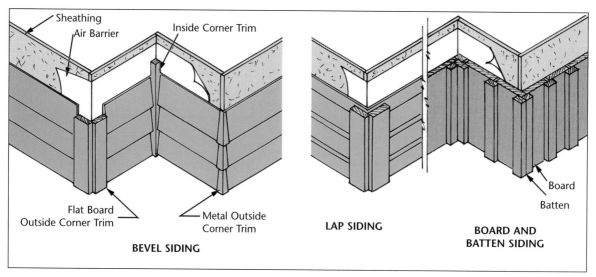

BEVEL SIDING
Sheathing
Air Barrier
Inside Corner Trim
Flat Board Outside Corner Trim
Metal Outside Corner Trim

LAP SIDING

BOARD AND BATTEN SIDING
Board
Batten

Figure 8.17 Inside and outside corners on wood siding can be trimmed with wood casings or metal corner covers

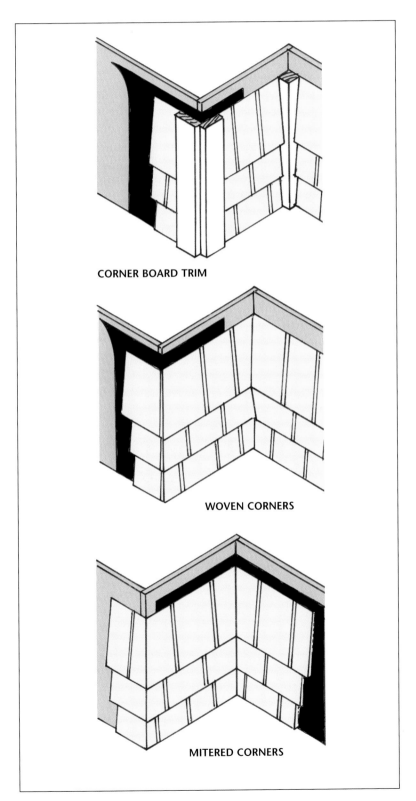

Figure 8.18 Wood shingle siding can turn corners by meeting corner trim or by mitering or weaving the shingles themselves.

CORNER BOARD TRIM

WOVEN CORNERS

MITERED CORNERS

Trimming Doors and Windows

Windows and doors are trimmed to the exterior finish material in various ways, depending on the finish material, sash material and desired appearance. Wood windows typically arrive on the jobsite with a pre-attached brick mold that both trims the outside and nails to the framing to hold the window in place. The sash of wood windows clad on the exterior with PVC or aluminum protrudes out past the sheathing, so that the siding can simply abut it with no additional trim. The joint between siding and sash is then caulked. However, the thin line of the exposed sash does not evoke the appearance of traditional windows. If this is desired, it can be had by adding a "window frame" trim around the sash. You can get a good idea of how various trim choices install with different door and window types by looking through the installation suggestions sections of manufacturers' catalogs. Some of the options are summarized in the following table.

DOOR AND WINDOW TRIM OPTIONS							
Sash Material	Exterior Finish			Trim Option			
	Wood siding, shingles, shakes	PVC (vinyl) siding	Brick, stone	Integral fin (no additional trim)	Pre-Applied brick mold	Pre-Applied flat (1x4) trim	Site-Applied trim
Doors							
Wood door sash	■				•		•
		▨			•		•
			▨		•		
PVC-clad wood door sash	■			•			•
		▨		•			
			▨	•			
Aluminum-clad wood door sash	■			•			•
		▨		•			
			▨	•			
Windows							
Wood windows	■				•		•
		▨			•		•
			▨		•		
PVC-clad wood windows	■			•			•
		▨		•			
			▨	•			
Aluminum-clad wood windows	■			•			•
		▨		•			
			▨	•			
PVC (all-vinyl) windows	■						•
		▨		•			
			▨	•			
Fiberglass (pultruded) windows	■			•			•
		▨		•			
			▨	•			

Figure 8.19 Wood windows come with the exterior trim piece already attached (top), which is nailed to the wall after the window has been positioned. Vinyl or aluminum clad windows (bottom) typically have a protruding trim attached to the outside of the frame and a nailing fin concealed beneath the siding.

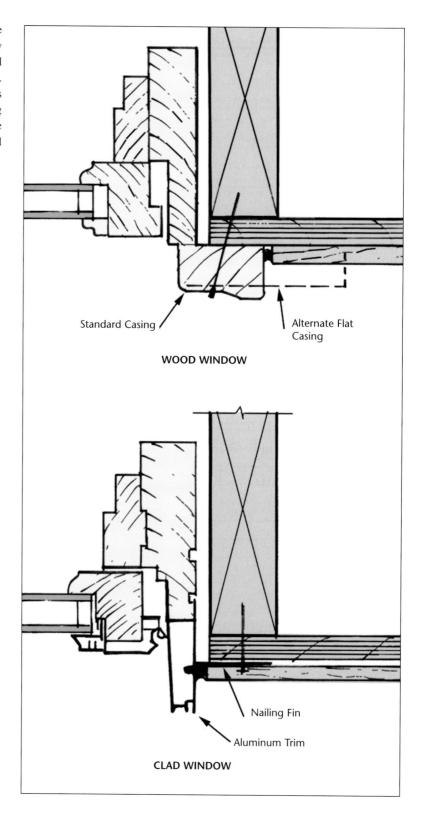

Standard Casing

Alternate Flat Casing

WOOD WINDOW

Nailing Fin

Aluminum Trim

CLAD WINDOW

CASE STUDY #2 –
REMOVING WALLS FOR A KITCHEN REMODEL

Much of the information we have learned about exterior walls comes to the forefront in the remodeling of a home in Utah. The owners decided to rethink their home to better suit their emerging needs as their two small children were getting older. They set four objectives for the design:

1. Replace the shared children's bedroom with two bedrooms in a new addition.

2. Create an acoustically private entertainment room.

3. Enlarge and open the kitchen.

4. Enclose the screen porch to create a dining room.

The existing U-shaped kitchen originally opened onto a dining room that adjoined the living room. The screened porch just outside the kitchen made a nice place to sit in the summer and enjoy the view of the Great Salt Lake in the distance but went unused for the rest of the year. Enlarging the kitchen entailed opening it into the porch, which would then become the new dining room. Removing the wall between the kitchen and abutting shared bedroom was easily done with no structural consequences. This was not the case, however, when it came to removing the exterior wall between the kitchen and screened porch and the wall segments between the kitchen and house. Because both of these were bearing walls, they were replaced with beams, properly sized to support the floor and roof loads above.

The formerly open screen wall of the porch was enclosed with an insulated stud wall and grouped casement windows that not only retained the views to the outside, but also open in warm weather for ventilation. The floor and ceiling of the porch were also insulated and finished to make a continuous weather envelope for the new dining room.

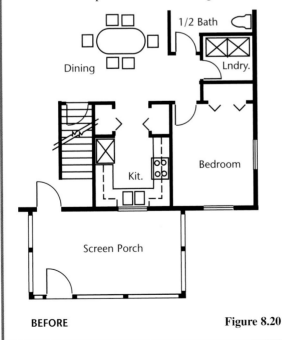

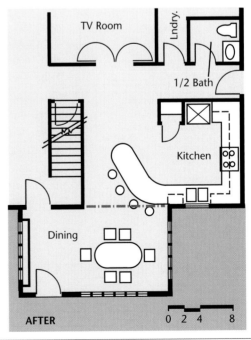

BEFORE   **Figure 8.20**   AFTER   0   2   4   8

CHAPTER 9: Doors and Windows

You probably pass through doors several times every day without thinking too much about them. And, you look out *through* windows, rather than at the windows themselves. Doors and windows constitute yet another important system of a home. In this case, the system is one of **access**. Doors provide controlled access from the outside to the inside and from space to space. Windows offer controlled access from the interior to light, view, ventilation and the warmth of the sun. In this chapter we'll see how to select doors and windows so that they provide the necessary kind of access.

DOOR TYPES

Doors are classified by the way they operate. Residential doors typically swing from hinges mounted in the side, or roll or slide sideways in tracks mounted in the head and sill.

Hinged Doors

Single-acting doors swing only in one direction, either inward or outward. **Double-acting doors** swing in both directions. You might need a double-acting door for a particular type of interior application but single-acting doors will probably account for the bulk of your kitchen and bath work. Single-acting doors hinge from one side and open on the other. They usually—but not always—open to the inside of the space accessed. Because doors can open from either side, as well as inward or outward, we need two terms to describe their operation. The first, the "**hand**," indicates the side where the hinges are located when you are standing outside. The second, "**reverse**," is used to designate doors that swing outward. There are four hands: right hand (RH), left hand (LH), right hand reverse (RHR) and left hand reverse (LHR). Though confusing, these tags are simpler if you imagine yourself facing the door from the outside (the side in which the key would be inserted).

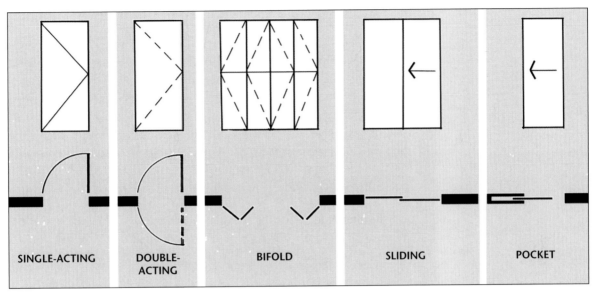

SINGLE-ACTING   DOUBLE-ACTING   BIFOLD   SLIDING   POCKET

Figure 9.1 Doors are classified by types, according to the way they open and close.

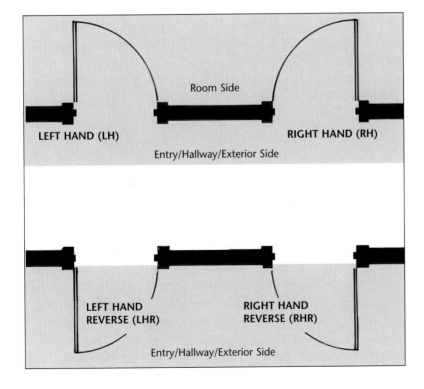

Figure 9.2 Single-acting doors are coded or "handed" by the direction in which they open into the room.

Room Side

LEFT HAND (LH)   RIGHT HAND (RH)

Entry/Hallway/Exterior Side

LEFT HAND REVERSE (LHR)   RIGHT HAND REVERSE (RHR)

Entry/Hallway/Exterior Side

Bifold Doors

Doors hinged from each other as well as from a jamb are called bifold doors. A pair of bifold doors actually contains four panels. The outer door of a bifold pair has a pin at the top that rides in a track, which aligns the doors as they open and close. Bifold doors suit locations where a single-hinged door would be cumbersome and places where you need a lot of access width, such as a wide closet. Two door panels, each 18 inches (457 mm) wide, create a pair of bifold doors for a 3-feet-wide (914 mm) opening. Wider openings up to 6 feet (1,829 mm) are possible by using sets of pairs (4 panels).

Sliding Doors

The second most common residential entry door type slides in tracks mounted in the head and sill (doors other than cabinet doors actually roll on rollers, rather than slide). Sliding doors can be installed in sets of two, three or four panels. Like bifold doors, sliders suit applications where more access width is needed than a hinged door offers or where space is too cramped for a hinged door to operate easily. The most frequent interior application for sliders is on a closet. Exterior sliding doors are usually glazed and called **patio doors** because they are most always used as a secondary access to a patio or deck. Kitchens often abut dining rooms that open onto decks. And if the trend for enclosed courtyards outside baths continues, expect to see more patio doors here as well.

Pocket Doors

Single doors can also slide, but instead of sliding past another door, they disappear into a pocket in the wall. When open this type of door is completely out of the way within the pocket. Pocket doors are especially useful in kitchen and bath areas where the door remains open much of the time or where a hinged door cramps the space. The door separating a dining room from a kitchen would be a possible location. Another would be a door to a private bath in a master bedroom suite. Pocket doors also sometimes allow easier access by people in wheelchairs. On the downside, the gain in unencumbered floor space is offset by the necessity for a pocket in the wall that must be kept clear of wires and pipes. If the wall is load bearing, a header significantly larger than a header for a single-wide door is needed. Pocket doors come in kits containing the track and assembly to be hidden in the wall pocket. There are kits that fit into interior walls framed with 2x4s.

DOOR STYLES

The term "style" is somewhat vague, but generally describes the construction and appearance of the door. Depending on the manufacturer the door styles described below are shipped as doors only—requiring a separate frame or pre-hung in frames. Pre-hung doors are generally preferred in residential work due to their simpler installation.

Flush Doors

The completely flat face of flush doors blends with contemporary houses but looks out of place in more traditional homes. Flush doors are available faced with hardboard for a paint finish or in various species of real wood veneers for a natural finish. There are two types of core construction. **Hollow-core (HC)**, the most economical, consists of a honeycomb of cardboard sandwiched between the face veneers. The stiles and rails are solid wood. Hollow core doors suit light-duty interior applications. They are not recommended for exterior doors. The sturdier and pricey **solid-core** (SC) doors, with a core made of wood staves, particleboard or other wood composition material, are used for exterior doors and interior doors subject to abuse or where the client wants quality or better sound control. They are also used between a kitchen and a garage when the code calls for a fire-rated door assembly.

Panel Doors

Traditional houses call for wood doors composed of solid wood panels set into stiles and rails glued together with mortise and tenon joinery, though **panel (stile-and-rail) doors** also blend well with modern-styled homes. Interior panel doors are typically 1 3/8 inches (35 mm) thick. Economy-class doors suitable for paint finish are made of fiberboard. Doors suitable for paint or natural finish are available in pine, fir and various hardwoods. Exterior doors are typically 1 3/4 inches (44 mm) thick. Panel doors come in various softwood and hardwood species suitable for paint or natural finish and in embossed hardboard, which needs to be painted. There are also exterior doors with embossed steel or fiberglass facings stamped with patterns to mimic true stile-and-rail panel doors. The facing material clads a wood or plastic foam core, the foam providing thermal insulation.

Exterior panel doors are available with solid or glazed panels in various patterns. Codes require all glazing in doors to be tempered glass for safety. Tempered glass, when broken, breaks into a multitude of small pieces, rather than irregular-shaped shards that can wound people by cutting or puncturing.

French Doors

Traditional French doors are paired doors that open inward or outward. The term "French door" has gotten somewhat muddled in recent years, with door manufacturers using it to cover a wide variety of glazed doors that include three- and four-door assemblies in "inswing" or "outswing" configurations. Three-door assemblies typically consist of a central operating door that hinges off one of the stationary side doors. In four-panel configurations, the two middle doors work as double-acting doors, hinged off the outboard door panels.

French doors are made up of a solid frame surrounding an array of glass panes separated from each other by narrow strips called **muntins**. Where the muntins truly separate individual panes, or lights, the glazing is called "**true divided light**." A newer, more energy-efficient version contains the muntin grid inside an unbroken insulated glass panel with secondary grids married to the inside and outside faces and is called "**simulated divided lights**." French doors are made of all wood or wood clad on the outside with aluminum or vinyl.

Patio Doors

As mentioned on page 108 under "Door Types" patio doors connect interior spaces with the outdoors, often opening onto patios, decks or courtyards. The simplest patio door contains two panels. The movable, or active panel is indicated with the letter "X," the inactive panel with the letter "O". Panel widths are 30 inches, 36 inches and 48 inches (762 mm, 914 mm, 1,219 mm), so the smallest single assembly would be 60 inches (1,524 mm) wide, using a pair of 30-inch (762 mm) leaves. The widest unit would be 12 feet (3,658 mm), made up of three 48-inch (1,219 mm)-wide leaves. Standard heights are 80 inches and 96 inches (2,032 mm, 2,438 mm). Units can be ganged together to create a glazed opening of any width.

Patio doors are available with frames of aluminum, wood or wood clad with vinyl or aluminum. Heat loss and gain is always a concern with exterior windows and doors and the frames of glazed doors offer many lineal feet of exposure. Wood or vinyl frames are fairly good insulators but aluminum is not. In winter, heat travels freely from the interior to the outside through the metal. If used in a wet area, such as a bath, moisture can condense on the inside and even turn to ice. The remedy is to specify door frames that have a non-conductive **thermal break** gasket sandwiched between the inside and outside portions of the frame.

Louvered and Mirrored Doors

Closet doors are often louvered to ventilate the interior or fronted with full-height mirrors. Bifold closet doors with louvers or mirrors are available in various widths. A louvered or mirrored hinged room door will probably have to be special ordered or custom fabricated.

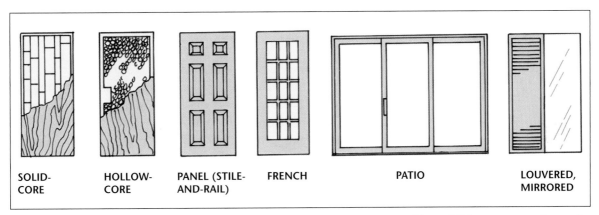

SOLID-CORE   HOLLOW-CORE   PANEL (STILE-AND-RAIL)   FRENCH   PATIO   LOUVERED, MIRRORED

Figure 9.3 Some common door styles used in residential construction.

Entrance Systems

The front door means more to the home than a way to get people in and out. As the principal arrival point for visitors, it requires design attributes that express its importance as a focal point of the house. Traditional homes often set their main entrance up a few steps into a porch, which accents the entrance and shelters visitors. Today's homes sometimes have a scaled-down version of a porch, with the front door built into an entrance system consisting of a door flanked by sidelights and topped with a transom window. Entrance systems come in a wide variety of configurations and material choices in pre-hung frames.

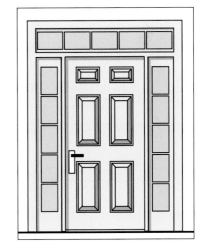

Figure 9.4 An entrance system combines one or more doors, flanking sidelights and transom windows into a single frame. Many styles and configurations are available.

RELOCATING DOORWAYS

Many interior alterations call for relocating the doors by opening a wall for a new door or closing off an old doorway. Creating a new door opening in an interior partition is fairly simple to do unless wiring and/or pipes are in the way. Re-routing wiring is usually feasible and not too costly. Re-routing pipes or ducts may not be possible and if it is, is sure to be expensive. Before finalizing your design, inspect the job to determine which of these might run through the proposed doorways. You can get a clue about the electrical from the location of outlets. Outlets on either side of the proposed opening are probably connected to wiring that runs through the area. You may be able to tell whether piping runs through the area by the location of existing fixtures. Check the floors below, for example, to see if there is a toilet. If so, its waste/vent pipe probably runs upward through the wall above. If, after your sleuthing, you still are not certain, have a portion of the wall finish removed from one side of the wall and peek into the cavity.

Interior bearing walls typically have double top plates. If this is the case, make sure you provide a header to take up the load of the structure above your new opening (See "Modifying Bearing Walls" in Chapter 12).

Closing off an existing doorway is simply a matter of removing the door, its hinges and casings, then filling the void with framing. A sole plate goes down on the floor, followed by trimmer studs nailed to the old jambs and one across the head to provide a nailer for the new wall finish. After one or two studs are installed in the center field, the opening is ready for the new wall finish material and base trim.

DOOR HARDWARE

Door hardware includes all of the parts that control movement of the door. It is called hardware because most of the parts are made of metal, though plastic is increasingly used for some interior parts of latch and locks, particularly in the economy lines. Hinges and pivots afford movement of swinging doors; rollers and tracks in sliding and bifold doors. For control of the movement there are push plates and various latchsets and locksets. Door closers, another controlling device, are rarely used in residential doors, so are not discussed here. Finally, there are accessories such as thresholds and doorstops.

Butts and Hinges

Though most of us call them **hinges**, this term technically refers to hardware mounted to the face of the door and frame. Most residential doors are hung on butts installed on the edge, or "butt" end of the door, exposing only the pin casing. Prehung doors come with butts already attached. Interior doors up to 36 inches wide typically require 1 1/2 pair (3 units) of butts, 3 1/2 inches x 3 1/2 inches (89 mm x 89 mm) in size. Double-acting door hinges have springs that return the door to the closed position. You can also get spring hinges for single-acting doors if you want them to be self-closing.

Locks and Latches

The hardware that controls the way the door is secured to the jamb opposite the butts is made up of a knob or lever and a mechanism to secure the door in place when it is closed. This assembly is called a **lockset**, if the door locks and a **latch**, if the door does not lock. The two most common types of locksets, by their construction, are **mortise locks** and **cylindrical locks**. Mortise locks are encased in a rectangular metal box that fits into a mortise carved out of the stile of the door. They are common in older houses, but have been pretty much superseded by cylindrical locks, which fit into a round hole. Cylindrical locksets offer many control options, which have names as well as a standard federal designation (ANSI number). Some of the more common ones you will most likely need in kitchen and bath installations are listed in the following table:

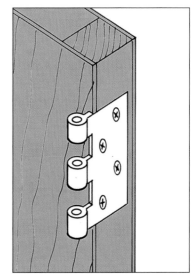

Figure 9.5 A door butt is a hinge that fits into a recess routed into the "butt" edge of the door.

Lock and Latch Functions			
ANSI Number	**Function Name**	**Description/Operation**	**Typical Locations**
F75	Passage Latch	Knobs both sides always unlocked.	Kitchen, walk-in closet
A20S	Closet Latch	Knob on corridor side, thumb turn inside, always unlocked.	Small closet
F76	Privacy Lock	Knobs both sides. Push-button on inside for locking. Releases by turning inside knob or opening from outside by inserting flat narrow tool in hole.	Bedroom, bathroom
F81	Entrance Lock	Knobs both sides, keyhole on outside knob, turn button on inside knob. Door locked by turning button and unlocked by turning inside knob or key from outside.	Entrance door
B252 E211	Security Deadbolt	Double cylinder deadlatch with latchbolt retracted by key from either side.	Entrance door

Lock and latch sets are available with knobs, levers or handles. Security deadbolts are used in addition to the primary lock/latch set for extra security at the main entrance. They are accessed by keys only. Levers are required in any job that must meet ADA accessibility standards and are a good idea in any door to be operated by an elderly or impaired person. Levers are gradually replacing round knobs for all doors because all users can more easily manipulate them. Handles are used on main entrance doors in tandem with thumb levers that control the latch.

Figure 9.6 Two types of locksets are commonly used in exterior residential doors: mortise locks (left) and cylindrical locks (right). Interior doors typically contain cylindrical locks or latchsets.

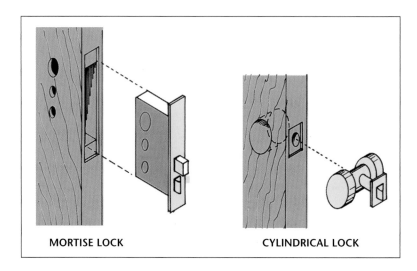

MORTISE LOCK   CYLINDRICAL LOCK

Figure 9.7 The parts of a quality cylindrical lock with a lever-type handle. (Courtesy of Schlage).

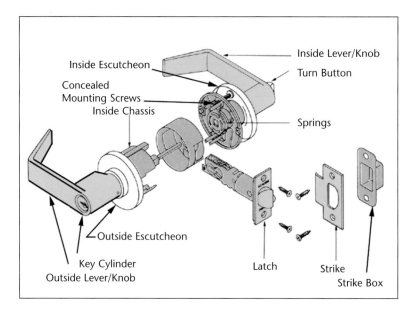

Inside Escutcheon

Concealed
Mounting Screws
Inside Chassis

Inside Lever/Knob

Turn Button

Springs

Outside Escutcheon

Key Cylinder
Outside Lever/Knob

Latch

Strike

Strike Box

SELECTING WINDOWS

Like doors, windows control access to interior spaces. Well-chosen, quality windows and skylights add both appeal and functionality to kitchens and baths by opening views to the outside, bringing in natural light and ventilation. Specifying windows to do these jobs well requires attention to several criteria. More often than not, no one window can satisfy all of the criteria equally well, so you will have to know enough about the tradeoffs to make the best compromise.

Appearance probably tops the list of criteria for your client, requiring choices of window type, sash material—both inside and outside—color and glazing configuration. The desired appearance may also establish the size and shape of the window, though these will more likely be determined by the space available and vertical location preferred. In recent years manufacturers have added numerous custom window shapes and muntin configurations to their standard lines, though options vary from one manufacturer to the other. Color choices are only by paint colors available with wood windows that have to be painted, but are more limited with windows clad with PVC or aluminum. White, beige and brown are options with most lines. Some offer other colors such as dark maroon and green. Glass, too, is available in blue, green or bronze tints, as well as clear. However, tinted glass affects energy performance, as we'll see under "Selecting Glazing," later on in this chapter.

WINDOW TYPES

All windows consist of a material that allows light to pass through, usually glass or plastic glazing set into a sash, which, in turn, fits into a frame affixed to the wall. The sash may be a simple surround consisting of horizontal rails and vertical stiles, or subdivided into a number of smaller panes by small pieces called muntins. We classify windows by type, according to how the sash opens and closes (operates).

Fixed Windows

Windows whose sashes don't open at all are called "fixed." Because fixed windows can't open they are poor choices for the only window in a kitchen or bath but may make an economical component of a multi-unit window assembly. Manufacturers typically offer fixed versions of their standard operating units but in more sizes, since size is not limited by the operating mechanism.

Double-Hung Windows

Vertical windows containing two operable sash units are fundamental to traditional colonial, cape and cottage-style homes. Both sashes of older, traditional double-hung windows moved up and down, suspended by ropes and counterweights concealed in the jambs. The ropes rode on pulleys in the top of the jamb, balancing the weights of the sashes so they stayed open at the desired position. These windows worked reliably for many years but have some downsides. Cleaning the outer panes from the inside is very difficult. The side pockets that contain the ropes-and-pulleys are a source of heat leaks. And, over time, the cords can break and require replacement. All of these problems have been solved in today's "tilt-turn" double-hung windows. Instead of ropes and pulleys, sashes glide up and down in weathertight jambs, held in place by friction and spring counterbalances. A latch at the top of each sash allows it to be tilted inward for easy cleaning from the room side.

Single-Hung Windows

Single-hung windows are a recent, more economical, product that works in the same manner as the newer double-hung windows, except that only the bottom sash operates. The top sash remains fixed in place. Having the upper sash fixed is a drawback only in applications where it is necessary to be able to open both sashes.

Sliding Windows

If you turn a double-hung window on its side, you have a sliding window (also called "gliding window"), except that the sashes can't be tilted inward for cleaning. The horizontal shape of sliders blends better with contemporary than traditional homes and is particularly well suited for kitchens and bath walls where an unobstructed lower wall is desired, such as above a tub/shower or above a kitchen sink. On the downside, the horizontal shape of sliding windows does not suit traditional-style homes.

Casement Windows

Casements are hinged at the sides to open outward and are controlled by a sill-mounted crank. Because the entire sash opens casements are the best choice for ventilation. They are made even more effective by the projecting sash that funnels passing breezes inside. Casements work well with modern-styled houses but also can suit traditional style homes if the sash is subdivided into several smaller panes (divided lights). Even with these advantages, some homeowners find the lack of a double sash inconsistent with their traditional-style homes, preferring double-hung windows.

Some manufacturers configure casement windows into assemblies that project out up to two feet from the wall of the house. **Box bay windows** have a rectangular footprint, whereas **angle bay windows** contain side windows on an angle of 30 or 45 degrees. The assemblies come with top and bottom platforms attached, needing only roofing on the top and trim and siding on the base to complete the installation. Bay windows are often the main kitchen window above the sink where the base and shelves provide platforms for plants.

Awning, Hopper and Jalousie Windows

If sliders are akin to double-hung windows turned sideways, awning windows resemble casements on their sides. They are hinged on the top and open outward from the bottom, allowing them to shed rain when open (unlike other types). Awning windows work well alone or as the vented units of a window group. Because they can take a long horizontal shape, awnings, like sliders, often make good choices above a tub/shower or kitchen sink. Stacked into vertical assemblies, awning windows become "hopper," or "projected" windows. Jalousie windows consist of several panes of glass hinged at the sides. Because the entire assembly opens this type works well where maximum ventilation is desired, which makes them popular in the South. On the downside, jalousie windows are a poor choice for cold climates. They are poor insulators because they are single glazed and have many cracks between the panes and at the sides.

Skylights and light tubes are not strictly windows but serve many of the same functions so are worth covering here.

Skylights

When windows can't be added, skylights can often be fitted into the roof to brighten up a dark portion of a room or bring light into a room with no window. Increasingly popular in homes, today's residential skylights look so much like residential windows they are often referred to as **roof windows**. Residential skylights are available with fixed or operating sashes that tilt outward to open. Frames and sash are usually made of wood and clad with aluminum or vinyl outside. Frames mount on a curb, usually built of 2x4s or included with the unit, or mount directly on the roof deck. Curb-mounted units don't visually blend in with the roof as snugly as deck-mounted ones, but are considered by many to be less prone to water penetration, since the skylight is raised above the roof surface. You can specify single- or double-glazing, along with low-e coating (described under "Selecting Glazing" on page 121). Operating blinds are also available for the underside of the frame. These control glare and reduce unwanted solar heat.

Light Tubes

Daylight not only illuminates rooms economically but cheers them as well. Until recently skylights provided the only way to bring daylight into landlocked interior rooms. Roof and ceiling configurations made even this difficult in some instances. Light tubes often offer a solution. They consist of a clear plastic dome on the roof connected to a highly reflective tube that terminates at the ceiling. Because the 10- to 14-inch-diameter tube is bendable it can be adjusted to install in difficult places without reframing the roof and building a light well as required for a skylight. The amount of light available from light tubes varies with their diameter and pathway shape. And, you can't see the sky through them, as with skylights.

Figure 9.8 As with doors, windows are classified according to the way they open and close. Because skylights used in residences so closely resemble windows, they are often called "roof windows". Recently introduced light tubes, while not strictly windows, offer a means of getting light through the ceilings of rooms with no outside windows.

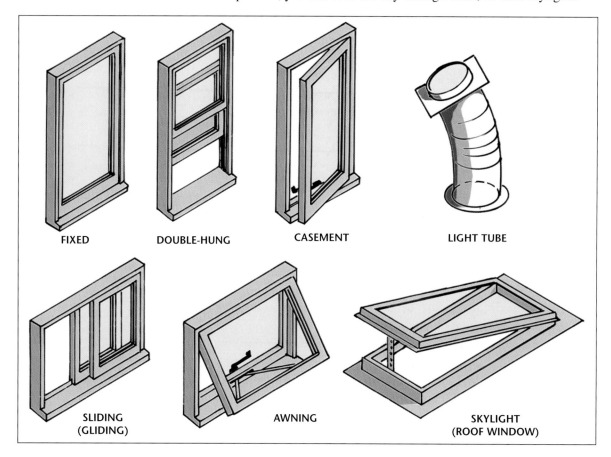

FIXED DOUBLE-HUNG CASEMENT LIGHT TUBE

SLIDING (GLIDING) AWNING SKYLIGHT (ROOF WINDOW)

SASH AND FRAME MATERIALS

Traditional window sashes and frames were made of wood, a material that was readily available and could be milled to make intricate profiles. Glass panes were held into the sash with linseed oil putty and the sash, frames and putty were painted after installation. In time, the paint chipped off, the putty hardened and the ensuing cracks created pathways for air and water leakage. Today's wood windows incorporate a host of technical improvements to address these problems including better design, improved sealants and exterior cladding materials, to name a few.

Pine is the wood of choice for most windows but other species, such as mahogany, are available where a natural finish or greater resistance to weather is desired. Wood windows clad on the exterior with PVC vinyl or aluminum offer the best of both worlds, the appearance of wood inside with a low-maintenance, weather-resistant skin outside.

Residential windows are also available made completely from materials other than wood, including aluminum or all-vinyl, in several factory-applied colors. In areas with cold winters, metal windows should contain a non-conductive thermal break material somewhere within the frame to stem heat flow through the metal. Without a thermal break the cold sash not only leaks heat to the outside, but also invites water to condense and run off onto the wall. Window sashes and frames made completely of vinyl are better heat insulators but look heavier than wood due to thicker sash and frame construction necessary for stiffness. Nonetheless, all-vinyl windows have been edging out all other types in recent years for both replacement and new window installations.

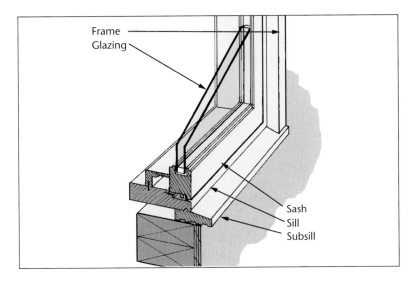

Figure 9.9 A typical double-glazed wood window mounted in a wood-framed wall.

Figure 9.10 Clad wood windows have exposed wood frames and sashes on the inside, vinyl (as shown) or aluminum cladding on the outside.

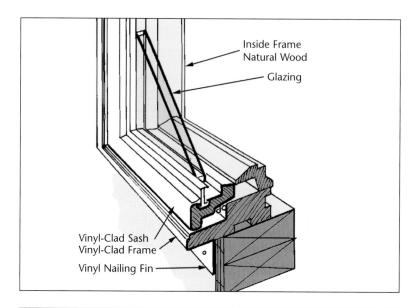

Inside Frame
Natural Wood

Glazing

Vinyl-Clad Sash
Vinyl-Clad Frame

Vinyl Nailing Fin

Figure 9.11 All-vinyl windows made their entrance into the residential market as replacement windows, but are now increasingly used as the prime window in new construction, thanks to their low cost, easy maintenance and high energy-efficiency rating.

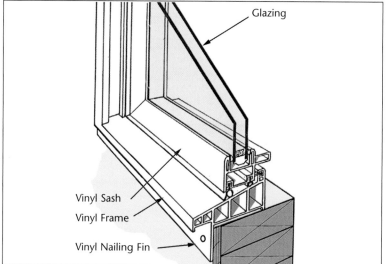

Glazing

Vinyl Sash

Vinyl Frame

Vinyl Nailing Fin

SELECTING GLAZING

The type of glazing you select for kitchen or bath windows affects heat gain and loss, as well as comfort, all of which are important to your client. A square foot of single-glazed window (R-1) wastes more than 19 times as much winter heat than an adjacent square foot of wall insulated to R-19. Adding a second pane to upgrade a single-glazed window to a double-pane (insulated) unit cuts this loss by half. The air space trapped between the panes doubles the insulating capacity of the window. Adding a third pane (triple-glazing) increases the R-value to around R-3; and a fourth pane (quadruple-glazing) to R-4. But adding more than two panes makes the window bulkier, heavier and costlier. And, if the window faces the sun, each successive layer cuts the amount of useful solar heat that comes through the glazing.

Three advances in recent years have made it possible to get high-performance windows with no more than two glass panes:

- Low-emissivity coatings

- Encapsulated membranes

- Inert gas fill

The first improvement is a microscopically thin metallic oxide coating called "low-e" (for low-emissivity) which controls solar heat gain and loss. Low-e coated windows allow various amounts of sunlight and heat to enter while preventing room heat from escaping back out. Coating one surface of a double-glazed window with low-e boosts its R-value from 2 to 3. Southern locations, where climate dictates the need for cooling, you'll need to block solar heat gain through the windows. With low-e coatings, you can control the amount of solar heat you want to admit or block by selecting the appropriate type of coating. Window suppliers can help you match the coating to the climate.

The second advance came with substituting thin sheets of coated polyester for glass for the inner panes of triple- and quadruple-glazed windows. The resulting glazing assembly achieves efficiencies up to R-8 without the added weight of two inner panes of glass.

Infusing a heavy gas such as argon and krypton into the dead air space between glazing layers yielded the third advance in window energy performance. Because these gases are more viscous than ambient air, they flow less within the glazing cavity, which reduces the heat transfer due to convectional movement.

None of these advances were possible without an airtight weather seal. State-of-the-art weatherstripping usually accompanies any new or replacement window. The weatherstripping is usually made of vinyl or EPDM plastic that stays flexible for several years.

Windows advertised as "high performance" vary in the features they are equipped with. So carefully examine the manufacturer's data for any windows you specify to make sure you get what you intend. However, convincing your clients that high-performance windows are in their best interest may take a bit of salesmanship. Not all homeowners are eager to pay a 10 to 15 percent premium for energy savings that may not be realized before 5 years or more. But, as energy costs continue to climb—as they are expected to—the "payback period" will decrease. And there are other benefits that begin immediately. Because low-e windows block heat radiated from the inside, they reflect back one's body heat, which results in better comfort. Also, low-e windows block the ultraviolet solar rays that fade carpets and furniture.

Figure 9.12 Many choices are available in high-performance glazing. Coating the interior surface of a double-glazed window (left) boosts the R-value from R-2 to R-3. R-values exceeding 5 are possible with windows containing low-e coated polyester films suspended between the two panes of glass (right) and filling the air spaces with heavy gases such as argon.

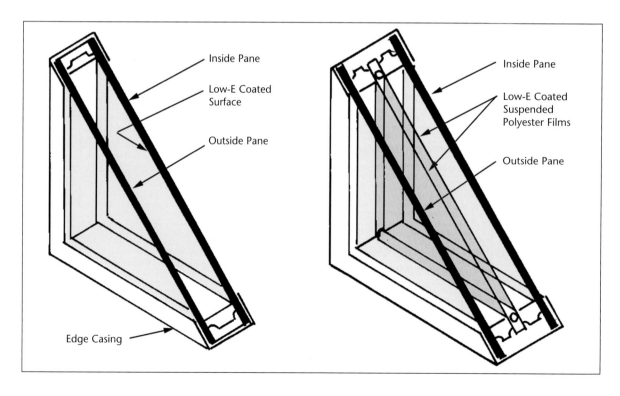

Inside Pane

Low-E Coated Surface

Outside Pane

Inside Pane

Low-E Coated Suspended Polyester Films

Outside Pane

Edge Casing

IMPROVING EXISTING WINDOWS

Any drafty windows you encounter on a remodeling job should be repaired, if possible, or replaced as part of the overall project. If, in addition to the air leaks around the sash, the windows are also single-glazed and the house is located in a cold-climate area, you should also recommend upgrading the glazing. You may be able to stem air leaks around the sash by specifying replacement weatherstripping. There are three ways to upgrade the glazing. From the most economical to most expensive they are:

1. Add storm windows to the exterior.

2. Install replacement sashes in the existing frames.

3. Replace the entire window unit.

Storm windows improve the energy efficiency of the basic window in proportion to its condition. The least efficient windows stand to gain the most from having a storm window added to the exterior. Units that are more efficient to begin with will see fewer gains. Storm windows are made to order, according to the size of the net opening inside the exterior window trim. They typically come with two glass panes and insect screens in a double-hung configuration mounted in aluminum tracks and are screwed to the window trim. The main benefit of storm windows is to block cold winds from the main window. Drawbacks include more difficult cleaning of the main windows and the fact that the storm window is what you see, for better or worse.

Replacement windows are a more energy-efficient way to improve leaky, single-glazed windows. They come in two basic forms. The first is a kit of parts containing the window sashes—wood, usually—and a set of jamb liners that fit into the existing window frames, after the old sashes and glass stops have been removed. Double-hung window replacement kits (the only type currently offered) contain an upper and lower sash unit and a jamb liner for each jamb. The jamb liners are made of vinyl and intended to replace the cumbersome pulley weights mounted in the side pockets of existing windows. Because replacement windows are manufactured in standard sizes, they may not fit the windows on your job.

Figure 9.13 A typical replacement window kit contains a top and bottom window sash and two vinyl jamb liners, along with the necessary clips and stops.

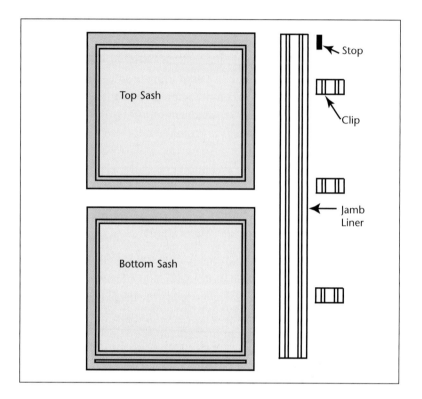

The second type of replacement window is an entire assembly made of all-vinyl windows. Like the kits just mentioned, these assemblies fit into the window opening after the old sash and glass stops have been removed. But unlike kits just mentioned, vinyl replacement windows are made to order to fit most any opening. Only double-hung window types are currently available. Glazing options are similar to new windows and include double-pane and low-e coating options.

Replacement of the entire window unit, the most expensive improvement, is necessary when the original window frame is in poor condition or the design calls for changing window size or location. Replacing entails removing all parts of the sash and frame of the existing unit and any enlargement or infill of the existing opening to accommodate the size and shape of the new window.

CASE STUDY #3 –
CREATIVE USE OF BATHROOM DOORS AND WINDOWS

A new bathroom in a Wisconsin house shows how windows can be effectively used—both inside and outside—to control access of persons, light and ventilation. The new bathroom is part of a master bedroom suite addition for a retired couple. A glass block wall around the toilet compartment creates privacy while allowing daylight to permeate the small space, replacing the claustrophobic feeling typical of these compartments with a cheerful openness. A similar glass block partition defines the shower compartment and curves around to keep water inside the shower and eliminate the need for a door or shower curtain.

Recessed medicine cabinets with mirror fronts flank the vanity cabinet in the center of the room. A small window placed above the vanity admits some daylight and fresh air into the room and affords the occupants a controlled view to the outdoors with minimum loss of privacy. Clerestory windows set into the cathedral ceiling flood the room with daylight but are high enough to ensure maximum privacy.

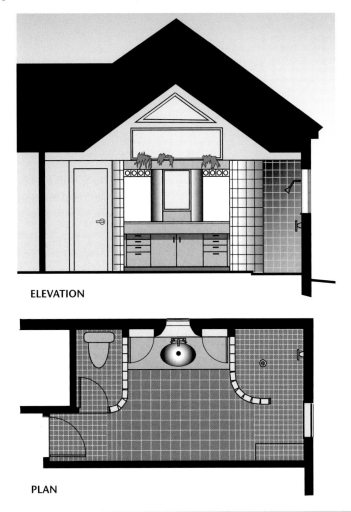

ELEVATION

PLAN

Figure 9.14

CHAPTER 10: Roofs

The roof is a home's first line of defense against the elements. Thermal insulation and a vapor barrier are just as important as a leak-proof weather skin to maintain comfort inside. And as part of the structural system of a house, the roof must be designed to withstand the wind, snow and seismic forces imposed on it without collapsing. Because the roof is bound to interface with your interiors at some point—such as in a skylight or light tube ceiling—you will need a general understanding of roof construction to effectively communicate with your client, contractors and architects.

ROOF FORMS

The shape of a roof is a good place to begin. Roof shapes follow regional home styles, influenced by the materials and technological capabilities of the region. They may be gable, hip, shed, flat butterfly, mansard, or gambrel, as shown in Figure 10.1. Interestingly, the fact that flat or nearly flat roofs are found in the dry Southwest as well as wetter Northwest and Northeast suggests that the ability to shed water is not a primary factor in roof form.

Gable, shed, mansard and hip roofs have a long history on houses. Because they all slope, they naturally shed water and do not leak if the roofing material is properly installed and maintained. Even sloped roofs thatched with grass can keep water out. The vulnerable spots in any sloping roof are the protrusions that interrupt the sloping planes. Each point at which a chimney, dormer or pipe pokes through the roof is a potential point for water to get in. Careful flashing, sealing and detailing is required to ensure that these points don't leak. **Flat roofs** and **butterfly roofs** do not, by their shape, shed water. In fact, they tend to entrap water. Special provisions needed to prevent leakage include an uninterrupted, continuous roof membrane equipped with roof drains at the interior portions and overflow scuppers at the edges.

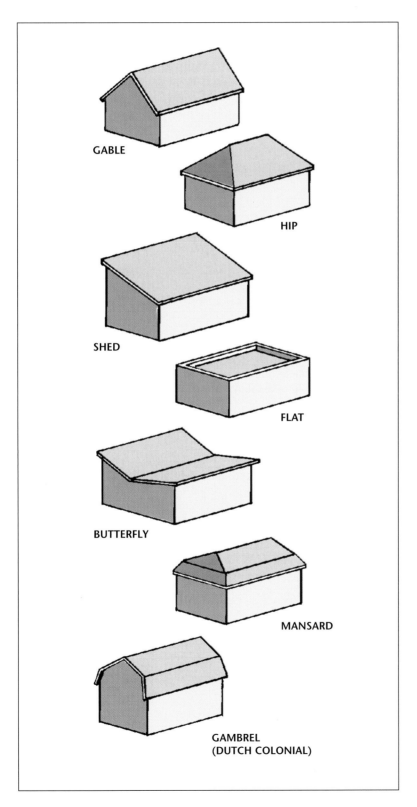

Figure 10.1 Some typical residential roof forms.

GABLE

HIP

SHED

FLAT

BUTTERFLY

MANSARD

GAMBREL
(DUTCH COLONIAL)

Now that you have an idea of the outside features of roofs, let's look inside to see how house roofs are constructed and how the roof construction relates to the rooms below. Except for post-and-beam houses (described in Chapter 9) most homes either have roofs framed of individual members—beams and rafters—or framed by trusses.

ROOF FRAMING SYSTEMS

Three structural systems account for most of today's residential roof framing. The following table gives a simplified overview of their differences

Framing System	Characteristics
Rafter Framing ("stick framing")	Many individual members (rafters), closely spaced, span between walls or beams. Spans limited to around 20 feet for sawn lumber; up to 30 feet with manufactured rafters ("I-joists").
Trusses	Several slender members assembled into triangular configurations make up trusses, which are usually spaced 24 inches apart to clear span up to 60 feet.
Panel Framing	Composite panels span up to 12 feet between trusses or timbers (in post-and-beam framing).

Rafter-Framed Roofs

Just as joists are long, slender members that span between supports in floors, rafters are the same for roofs. In **flat roofs** the rafters lie flat or nearly flat to span between beams and/or outer walls. Rafters in **shed roofs** span similarly except with greater slope. A shed roof is less common as the main roof of the house than as the roof of an addition, where the rafters span from a new outer wall to bear on the roof of the main house or onto a ledger set on one of the walls of the house, as shown in Figure 10.2. Shed roofs are also one roof form for dormer windows (Figure 10.3), where they increase headroom and provide an opportunity for windows in an otherwise too shallow attic.

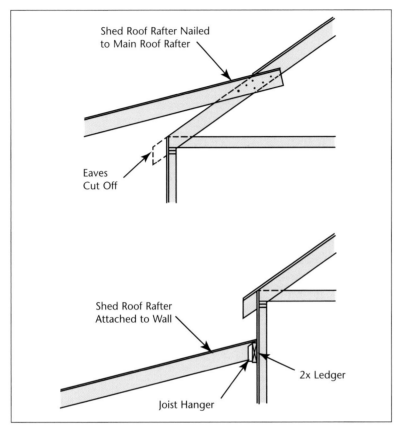

Figure 10.2 Shed roofs can frame into the main structure at the roof plane (top) or into a side wall (bottom).

Shed Roof Rafter Nailed to Main Roof Rafter

Eaves Cut Off

Shed Roof Rafter Attached to Wall

Joist Hanger

2x Ledger

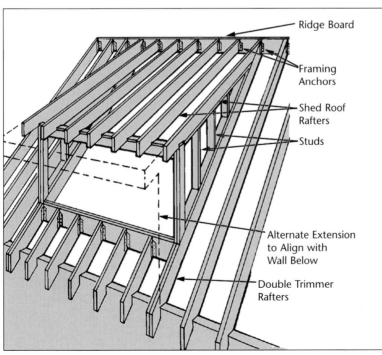

Figure 10.3 Shed roof dormers can spring from the ridge of the roof, as shown, or from a point downslope. The front wall can recess behind the wall below it or extend out to the plane of the wall. Note that all framing members around the roof opening are doubled.

Ridge Board

Framing Anchors

Shed Roof Rafters

Studs

Alternate Extension to Align with Wall Below

Double Trimmer Rafters

Roofs that slope downward from a central ridge, gable roofs, are the most common form for the main roof of most houses. Framing a **gable roof** with rafters is a little more complicated than framing over a shed roof, because the system must resist an outward force, or thrust, in addition to the vertical loads of the roof. Horizontal members, or ties, between the rafters are used to resist the outward thrust by tying them together to keep the walls from spreading. The lower the ties, the more effective they are. Ties can be the attic floor joists, if they are continuously tied together across its span and secured to the ends of the rafters. Placed higher up, they are called "collar ties." but they must be located in the lower third of the roof in order to be of any use in resisting thrust. This presents a dilemma in attics designed for occupancy, since placing the ties low reduces the headroom.

Another way to counter thrust in gable and hipped roofs is by supporting the rafters at the ridge with a **bearing wall** or **ridge beam**, either below the rafters or in the same plane (face framed), as shown in Figure 10.5. The ridge beam, in turn, spans between columns or walls. While a ridge beam takes on the vertical load of the rafter ends that frame into it, it shouldn't be confused with a **ridge board**, which takes no vertical load, but merely provides a convenient nailer for installing the rafters. Also, your code may require a ridge board or blocking between the framing to help the roof act as a diaphragm in resisting wind or seismic forces. Gable roofs are also used above gable (or "doghouse") dormers, framed as shown in Figure 10.7.

Figure 10.4 The outward thrust of a pitched roof can be countered by collar ties between the rafters or by the attic floor joists, if care is taken to ensure structural continuity, end to end (left). The attic floor can't be used in attics with kneewalls (right).

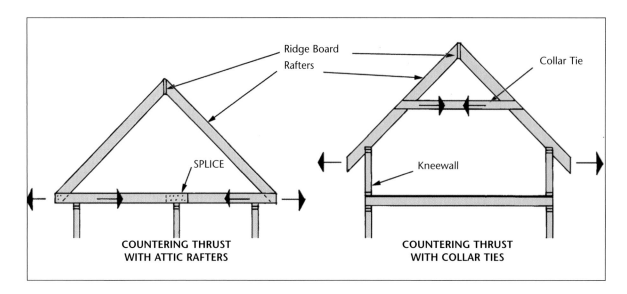

COUNTERING THRUST
WITH ATTIC RAFTERS

COUNTERING THRUST
WITH COLLAR TIES

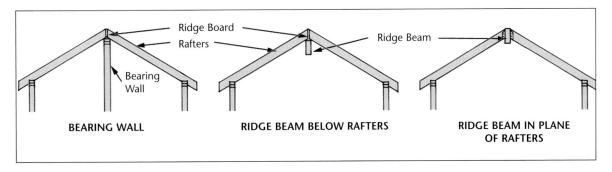

Figure 10.5 Supports directly below the ridge offer an alternative way to counter outward thrust in pitched roofs. The supports can be a bearing wall or beam at the ridge.

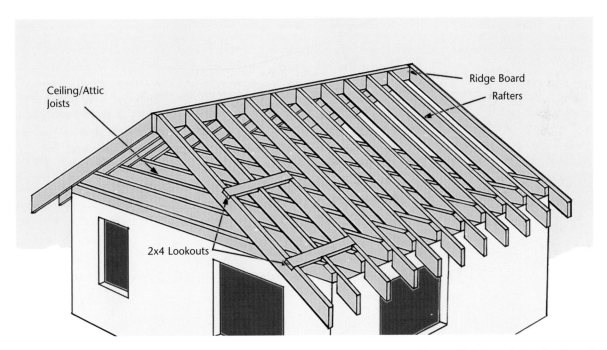

Figure 10.6 A typical rafter-framed gable roof. Lookouts (cross pieces set into the end rafters) support the rake (outside rafter) at the gable ends.

Figure 10.7 Framing a gable ("doghouse") dormer begins with a double-framed opening in the roof plane. As with shed roof dormers, the front wall can sit back or above the wall below.

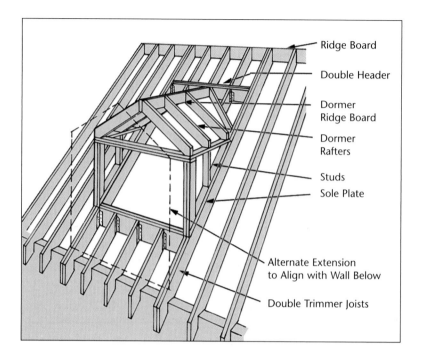

- Ridge Board
- Double Header
- Dormer Ridge Board
- Dormer Rafters
- Studs
- Sole Plate
- Alternate Extension to Align with Wall Below
- Double Trimmer Joists

Sizing Rafters

Rafters are sized according to the loads they carry and their spacing. Rafters are usually spaced 12, 16 or 24 inches (305 mm, 406 mm, 610 mm) apart. These spacing modules fit standard sheathing panel sizes and span ratings for 1/2-inch (13 mm) and 5/8-inch (16 mm)-thick sheathing. Rafters must be stiff enough to support their loads without sagging excessively (deflection). Allowable deflection for rafters that do not have ceilings attached to their underside is usually limited to 1/240 of the span (L/240). If the ceiling is attached the deflection should be limited to 1/360 of the span to prevent cracking of the plaster or drywall ceiling (The span for rafters on a sloped roof is the projected horizontal distance between supports rather than their actual length).

As with floor joists, rafters carry two different kinds of loads: live loads and dead loads. Live loads for roofs come from wind and snow and vary from region to region. If you are sizing rafters yourself you can find out the appropriate live loads from the local building inspection department. For dead loads, allow 5 to 8 psf (0.34 kN/m² to 0.38 kN/m²) for light framing with shingle roofing and 8 to 14 psf (0.38kN/m² to 0.67 kN/m²) for tile or slate roofing. (Always verify with the material specifications). Once you have determined the spans, spacings, loading and allowable deflection, you can select rafters from span tables published by lumber trade associations, following the procedure described for selecting floor joists in Chapter 7. The table below, "Rafter Selection," is an example.

Size	Spacing (inches on center)	Grade and Spacing (feet and inches)							
		Dense Select Structural	Select Structural	Non-Dense Select	No. 1	No. 1 Non-Dense	No. 2	No. 2 Non-Dense	No. 3
2x6	12	13-0	12-9	12-6	12-6	12-3	12-3	11-9	10-0
	16	11-10	11-7	11-5	11-5	11-2	11-2	10-8	8-8
	24	10-4	10-2	9-11	9-11	9-9	9-1	8-9	7-1
2x8	12	17-2	16-10	16-6	16-6	16-2	16-2	15-6	12-9
	16	15-7	15-3	15-0	15-0	14-8	14-5	13-10	11-0
	24	13-7	13-4	13-1	13-1	12-6	11-10	11-3	9-0
2x10	12	21-10	21-6	21-1	21-1	20-8	19-11	18-11	15-1
	16	19-10	19-6	19-2	19-2	18-5	17-3	16-5	13-0
	24	17-4	17-0	16-9	15-8	15-1	14-1	13-5	10-8
2x12	12	26-0	26-0	25-7	25-7	25-1	20-2	19-5	15-6
	16	24-2	23-9	23-3	22-10	21-11	20-2	19-5	15-6
	24	21-1	20-9	20-4	18-8	17-11	16-6	15-10	12-8

RAFTER SELECTION
Southern Pine, 40 psf live load, 10 psf dead load, deflection limited to 1/240

"Rafter Selection" excerpted from *Maximum Spans: Southern Pine Joists & Rafters*, published by the Southern Pine Marketing Council.

Trussed Roofs

Loads imposed perpendicular to the long length of the rafters and beams cause them to bend or deflect. The rafters must be stiff enough to resist these forces. But there is another approach that eliminates bending: organize the roof framing into a series of triangles in the form of **trusses**. Because triangles are inherently stable, the same amount of material can be re-allocated to support a greater load. Instead of pressing against the long side of the framing member causing it to bend, the load pushes or pulls at each end, resulting in pure tension or pure compression. Lightweight, prefabricated trusses are widely used in residential roofs. The most common consist of 2x4s and/or 2x6s connected by sheet metal plates (gussets). Trusses made of light-gauge metal are also increasing in use. While trusses cost more, in material terms, than rafters and beams, they save enormously in labor because they are prefabricated in a factory and arrive on the job ready to pop up into place. The labor savings increase with the number of trusses used. Another big advantage of trusses is their ability to span greater distances between supports. Trusses easily span the total width of a typical house, 25 to 40 feet (7,620 mm to 12,192 mm), leaving the space below completely open and flexible for use as living or storage space.

Prefabricated trusses are typically spaced 24 inches (610 mm) apart. That's about the only constant, since they can be designed and fabricated in almost any shape that can be subdivided into triangles. This advantage alone makes them useful for framing spaces with unusual ceiling geometry. The simple gable form truss is the most economical shape to roof an interior that has a flat ceiling. But if your job calls for a sloped ceiling, you can get a truss with a scissors shape. Another truss shape suits a roof where one side has a different slope than the other. Trusses can also be shaped to accommodate thicker insulation or wide openings. Stepped trusses allow framing a hipped roof without additional stick framing. Truss suppliers are usually willing to discuss your requirements at an early stage in the project and make suggestions for the best solution.

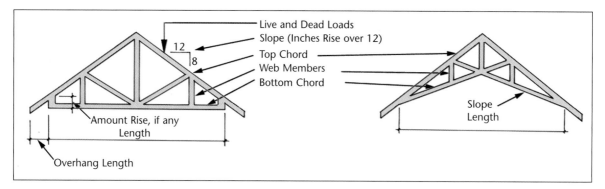

Figure 10.8 Prefabricated, engineered, lightweight, roof trusses can be made in many shapes and span openings up to 40 feet (12,192 mm). When ordering, you must provide the live and dead loads, slope (rise and run), length and overhang. They must be ordered to exact length and cannot be altered on the job.

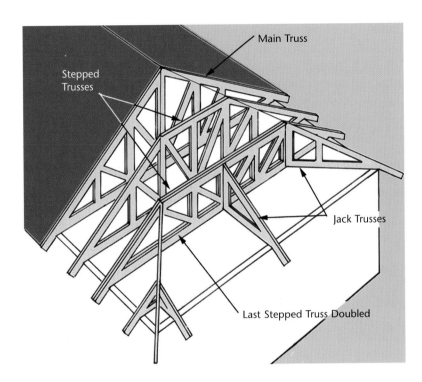

Stepped Trusses

Main Truss

Jack Trusses

Last Stepped Truss Doubled

Figure 10.9 Hipped roofs can be framed with rafters or special trusses, each of which has a different profile.

Panel Roofs

Post-and-beam framing and roofs framed with widely-spaced, heavy trusses are often clad with **structural insulated panels (SIPs)** as mentioned in connection to walls in post-and-beam houses in Chapter 9. These composite sandwiches of sheathing/foam/sheathing not only serve as the sheathing of the roof and the insulation system, but also provide a nail-base material on the inside for attaching the ceiling. Most SIPs can span up to 48 inches on the roof. In post-and-beam houses where the members are typically spaced at 8-, 10-, or 12-foot (2,438 mm, 3,048 mm, 3,658 mm) intervals, purlins (sub framing members) are placed across the roof beams 48 inches (1,219 mm) apart (see Figure 8.2).

Roofs with Cathedral Ceilings

Varying ceiling heights from one room to the next can add importance to certain rooms and make the house a more interesting grouping of spaces. One way to do this is by raising ceilings in some rooms and lowering them in others. Another is to have the finish material hug the underside of the sloping roof structure to form a **cathedral ceiling**. Any of the three framing systems described above can be used to frame a cathedral ceiling. In **rafter systems** the ceiling material is simply attached to the underside of the rafters. Similarly, the interior sheathing of an SIP roof becomes the substrate for the ceiling. In **trussed roofs**, the trusses must be configured into a shape with a pitched bottom chord (the member of the truss abutting the ceiling). Scissors trusses offer a way to do this.

Figure 10.10 Three ways to frame and insulate a cathedral ceiling.

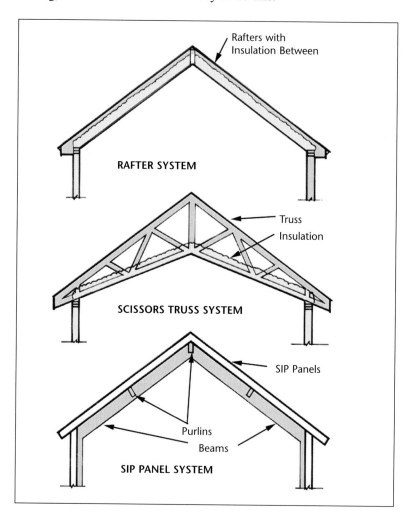

RAFTER SYSTEM

Rafters with Insulation Between

SCISSORS TRUSS SYSTEM

Truss
Insulation

SIP PANEL SYSTEM

SIP Panels

Purlins
Beams

ROOF SHEATHING MATERIALS

The OSB that makes the top of an SIP sandwich becomes the **sheathing** layer. It supports the live and dead loads imposed on the roof and provides a base for the roofing material. Rafter- and truss-framed roofs require a separate sheathing layer. Solid boards laid across the main framing served this purpose in houses built before the advent of panel sheathing. Most roofs are now sheathed with solid panels of plywood or OSB, 1/2 inch (13 mm) or 5/8 inches (16 mm) thick, installed with the long panel dimension running across the framing. When specifying roof sheathing make sure the material is rated for the rafter or truss spacing. Roofing felt, a material consisting of organic fibers pressed together in a bituminous matrix, is recommended for an underlayment for most types of roofing. It is installed with roofing nails and sheet metal washers. In areas with severe winters an additional strip of elastomeric material (ice shield) is often added at the eaves for extra protection against water penetration.

INSULATION AND MOISTURE CONTROL

As with walls, roofs in all climates must be insulated to control heat loss and gain. Also, the thermal insulation must be coordinated with a moisture control strategy. This is especially important for roofs above kitchens and baths, which generate more moisture than other rooms.

Where you place the insulation depends on the shape of the roof structure and use of the space inside. For a cathedral ceiling attached to the underside of the roof framing the insulation can go in the cavities of the framing above the roof sheathing, between the framing and ceiling or in some combination.

Houses with attics offer different options. If the attic is sealed off or only used for storage, the insulation can go in the attic floor. For occupied attics, where the space will be heated and/or cooled the insulation must be placed above and around the sides of the occupied space. If you have a choice insulating the attic floor is easier and more economical than fitting insulation between rafters and sidewalls and allows the attic to be ventilated from the outside.

Ventilation of the air space between the insulation and roof surface has two advantages. First, it keeps the roof cooler, year round, thus extending the life of the roofing material. Second, ventilation prevents ice dams at the eaves in cold climates. In winter a roof that stays cold prevents alternate freezing and thawing of ice, which leads to ice dams that cause water to penetrate the roof.

137

To ventilate the roof surface you must provide a pathway of outside air just under the sheathing. The entire attic space serves as the airspace in an open attic. In a closed attic the airspace must be located somewhere within the rafters. The best place is between the insulation and roof sheathing. The airspace should be at least two inches deep. It can be achieved by installing foam plastic insulation baffles on the underside of the roof sheathing prior to installing the cavity insulation.

As stated for walls, humidity is higher indoors in winter than the colder, drier air outside. As the warm, moist air migrates through the building envelope—in this case the roof/ceiling—it can condense to cause deterioration of the framing members and ceiling finish. The first line of defense against this moisture is a good vapor barrier, usually a layer of 4- or 6-mil polyethylene sheet, installed between the insulation and the ceiling finish. If foil-faced foam insulation is used, as it might be in a cathedral ceiling, the joints can be taped to make a good vapor barrier.

Figure 10.11 A "cold" roof system contains the insulation on the attic floor. Vents in the soffit and ridge prevent moisture buildup in the attic. If a ridge vent is not feasible, other means of evacuating the air may be used, such as gable vents (inset).

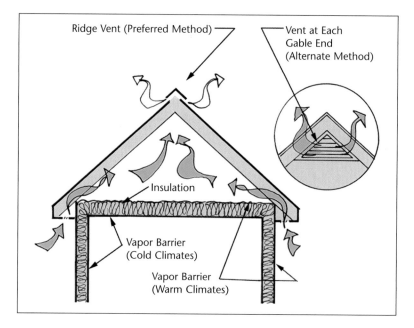

Ridge Vent (Preferred Method)

Vent at Each Gable End (Alternate Method)

Insulation

Vapor Barrier (Cold Climates)

Vapor Barrier (Warm Climates)

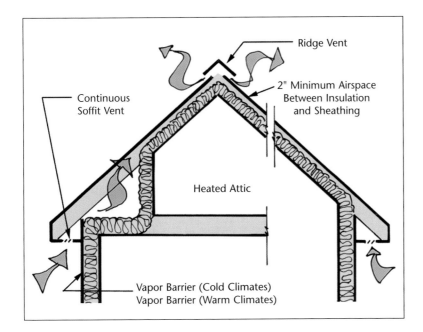

Figure 10.12 Occupied attics and cathedral ceiling roofs require insulation around the heated space. Note that a 2-inch (51 mm) airspace is required between the insulation and roof sheathing to ensure adequate circulation.

ROOFING

The weather "skin" atop the house must be selected with care to meet several criteria: initial cost, durability, resistance to wind and fire and local code requirements. And because most residential roofs slope to shed water they are highly visible so appearance is generally an important consideration as well. The color, texture and pattern of the roofing must blend with the house for a successful job. Last but not least, roofing must shed water unfailingly. Below are brief descriptions of each roofing material option followed by a table that compares them in summary form.

Wood Shingles and Shakes

Cedar and redwood shingles, common home roofing materials prior to the 1940s, now cost so much that they are out of reach of many homeowners. Still, you may need to consider wood shingles for a kitchen or bath addition to match the main house. First, evaluate the condition of the present shingles. If they are in poor shape, it might make more sense to re-roof, which opens the possibility of using another material. Even if the existing shingles are sound, new shingles on the addition will take a few years to gray enough to match their color.

Wood shingles today are usually installed over plywood or OSB sheathing that has been covered with a layer of roofing felt. Shingles are either applied directly over the felt or to 1x3 strapping (furring strips) attached horizontally over the felt at the same spacing as the shingle exposure, usually 5 1/2 inches (140 mm). Recently introduced "shingle breather" materials, available in rolls, are an alternative to strapping. This method allows the undersides of the shingles to breathe, which prolongs their life. The first shingle course is doubled and projects 2 inches (51 mm) over the drip edge.

Figure 10.13 Wood shingles are typically installed on strapping the same distance apart as the shingle exposure to prevent entrapped moisture on the undersides of the shingles. Saturated felt below the strapping provides a backup water barrier.

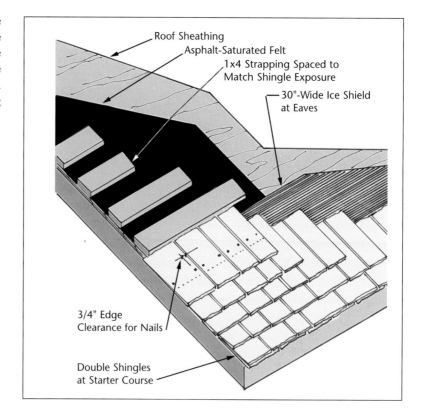

Roof Sheathing
Asphalt-Saturated Felt
1x4 Strapping Spaced to Match Shingle Exposure
30"-Wide Ice Shield at Eaves
3/4" Edge Clearance for Nails
Double Shingles at Starter Course

Asphalt and Fiberglass Shingles

Asphalt-based shingles reign as the most popular roofing for today's homes because of their low cost, wide range of colors, patterns and textures and the ease of installation and repair. Traditional asphalt shingles consist of an organic fiber mat saturated with asphalt and topped with mineral granules.

Fiberglass replaces the organic mat in so-called "fiberglass" shingles, saving weight and petroleum. Though stronger than their heavier forerunners, the first generation of fiberglass shingles didn't seal as well as asphalt and tended to blow off in a heavy wind. Today's products have reportedly corrected this shortcoming.

Both types come in profiles ranging from flat to textured, with colored, mineral surface granules in tans, greens, red, grays and black. The textured varieties achieve a sculptured look by alternating thicker (laminated) layers with single layers of material. As with wood shingles, asphalt and fiberglass shingles are nailed to the sheathing over a layer of roofing felt. The starter strip is doubled and for extra protection in damp locations, set over a strip of bituminous water/ice shield. Shingles are normally spaced at 5 inches.

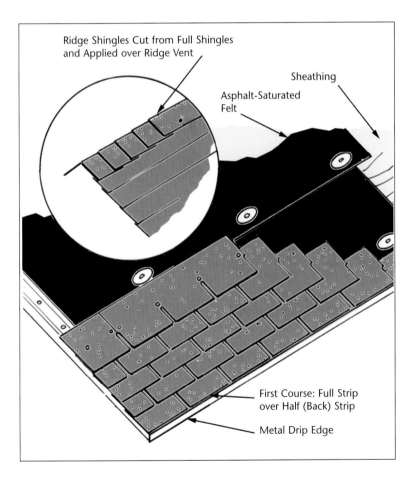

Figure 10.14 Asphalt and fiberglass shingles install over a layer of felt. Form ridges (inset) by cutting shingles sideways and nailing along the sides.

Metal Roofing

Metal roofing, previously associated with commercial and industrial buildings, is now coming into its own as a high-end residential material. The best metal roofing is made of terne, an alloy of metal and copper. Less costly options in steel and aluminum are available in a wide range of baked-enamel colors. At this time, 24-inch-wide panels in lengths up to 18-feet long make up the bulk of residential metal roofing.

Metal roofing panels are connected to the roof deck by metal clips attached to the edges on the long sides. The edges are raised in various shapes to conceal the fasteners and overlap the adjacent panel for a weather seal. Smaller ribs run down the middle section of the panels to prevent dimpling. Special shapes are required at ridges, changes of directions and intersections with protrusions, such as dormers and chimneys. These details always stand out and often look awkward, making metal roofing a better candidate for simple roof forms rather than for those with complicated shapes or a lot of protrusions.

Figure 10.15 Metal roofing, once used only in commercial and industrial buildings, now tops many residences. Many profiles and colors are available.

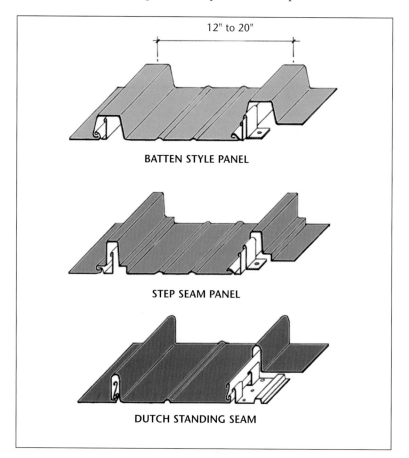

12" to 20"

BATTEN STYLE PANEL

STEP SEAM PANEL

DUTCH STANDING SEAM

Slate

Natural slate is a high quality roofing material that has been in use for centuries. Installed properly, it can last for centuries. Roofing slate is quarried from beds and split into thin sheets. Their natural, irregular shapes have subtle color variations ranging from blacks and grays to blues and greens—some even include reds and browns. Slate is also fireproof.

On the downside, its brittleness makes it a poor choice in a hurricane-prone area or under a large tree that can drop limbs off from time to time. Standard slates are 12 inches x 16 inches and 14 inches x 20 inches (305 mm x 406 mm and 356 mm x 508 mm) 3/16- or 1/4-inch (5 mm or 6 mm) thick. Sheets vary somewhat from these target dimensions. Each slate is laid over a wood deck covered with roofing felt and secured with two copper nails. Copper wire and roofing cement secure pieces near ridges and hips. A cant strip is installed under the starter course to give it the same pitch as successive courses.

Roofing Tiles

Clay tiles have been in use ever since sun-baked clay tiles topped the roofs of the houses of ancient Crete. Today's fired clay tiles impart the Mediterranean look so common to the stucco homes of California and Florida. Clay tiles come in various profiles and earth-based colors. In addition to clay tiles made by fusing the material together in a kiln, there are other tiles made by other processes, such as concrete tiles made with Portland cement.

All tile roofs are durable, long lasting and fireproof and are excellent at shedding water. On the downside, tiles impose a hefty dead load requiring a structure capable of carrying the added weight of around 14 psf ($0.67kN/m^2$). Tiles, like slates, are brittle materials that are vulnerable to damage from wind-borne objects and earthquakes. Tiles install over felt-topped roof sheathing, anchored with ring-shank nails or screws over roofs with slopes of at least 3:12. Local codes in high-wind areas may require hurricane clips at ridges and eaves. Metal flashing seals joints at intersections with walls. Mortar is used at ridges and roof bends.

Single Membrane Roofs

Flat roofs and roofs under upper-story balconies are often roofed with a single membrane made of elastomeric materials such as EPDM or neoprene. The roof membrane bonds to the roof either by mechanical anchors or adhesive, or it can be loosely laid and held in place by gravel. This type of roofing has all but replaced traditional hot-mopped asphalt used on low-slope roofs, due to its ease of installation and longer life.

COMPARING ROOFING MATERIALS						
	Asphalt Shingles	Wood Shingles	Metal	Tile	Slate	Membrane Roofing
Minimum roof slope (inches rise per foot horizontal)	3:12 2:12[1]	4:12	2 1/2:12	4 1/2:12[3] 2 1/2:12[3]	6:12	(None)
Material cost	Low	Medium	Medium	High	High	High
Installation cost	Low	Medium	Medium	Medium	High	Medium
Life span, years	15-20	10-40	15-40+	20+	30-100	15-30
Weight, psf[4]	2.25 to 3.85	3 to 4	0.5 to 2.7	3.75 to 11	5 to 10	2 to 104
Fire rating[2]	A	B	A	A	A	A

[1]2:12 slope requires installation for "low-slope" applications.
[2]An "A" rating is best. Wood shingles and shakes are treated with a fire retardant and rated "B". Untreated wood shingles and shakes, combustible, carry no fire rating.
[3]Clay tiles require a minimum slope of 4 1/4:12; cement tiles can go down to 2 1/2:12.
[4]Higher values are for systems using gravel ballast.

ROOF EDGES

What happens at the eaves and intersections with another surface or object can be more important to the appearance and function of the roof than the roofing material itself. Because these points interrupt the continuity of the roof they are the areas most vulnerable to leaks. Keeping water out requires adequate **flashing** and **sealing** at each intersection with an adjoining roof surface, wall, chimney and vent pipe. The roofing itself might suffice for some terminations. For example, asphalt shingles can be bent around the ridges and valleys of a hipped roof with no additional flashing material. But more typically, these junctions require separate flashing material formed into a special shape. Copper is the best all-purpose flashing for quality roofs of wood shingles, slate or tiles. Aluminum, galvanized steel and PVC are also used. Nails for metal flashing must be chosen to resist rust as well as corrosion through contact with a dissimilar flashing metal. Copper nails are used with copper; aluminum with aluminum. Steel nails pair with galvanized steel and vinyl flashing. Unless steel nails are made of stainless steel (the best choice), they should be coated by hot-dipped galvanizing.

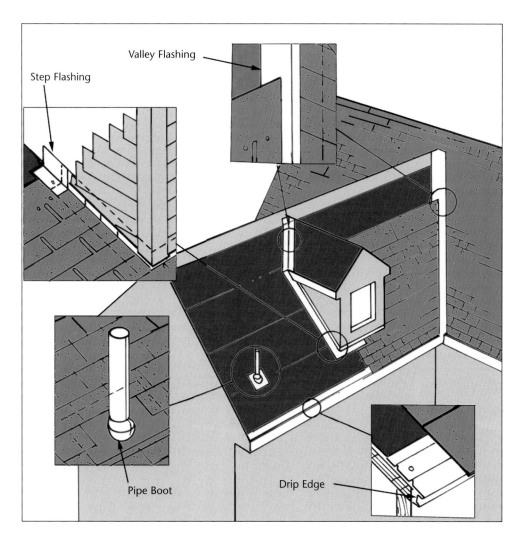

Step Flashing

Valley Flashing

Pipe Boot

Drip Edge

Figure 10.16 Roofs must be properly flashed wherever the roofing is interrupted or abuts another surface. Some critical locations are shown here.

CASE STUDY #4 –
A CATHEDRAL CEILING KITCHEN ADDITION

A Saskatchewan kitchen addition shows how a well-conceived roof can unite a house and detached garage. The narrow, pie-shaped site meant the garage was set at an angle to the house, separated by an unattractive, cramped courtyard. In winter the courtyard filled with snow making passage between the garage and house difficult. When the owners set out to expand the house the designer suggested tying the two buildings together with an addition. Her scheme placed the kitchen and dining areas in the addition so that both rooms could have views to the outside.

The key to making a practical and visually successful transition from the single-story garage to the two-story house was the roof of the addition, whose ridge ran at right angles into both the wall of the house on the one side and the garage roof on the other. Because the addition was a one-story structure, it offered the possibility of a cathedral ceiling for more interesting kitchen and dining areas. The designer seized the opportunity by framing the rafters into a ridge beam that spanned between the house and garage. Insulation occurs between the rafters. A gap above the insulation provides a pathway for air to circulate, entering through vents in the eaves and exiting through the ridge vent. The gypsum wallboard ceiling slopes downward from the ridge beam to a level soffit above the counters. The soffit houses recessed lights that illuminate work surfaces.

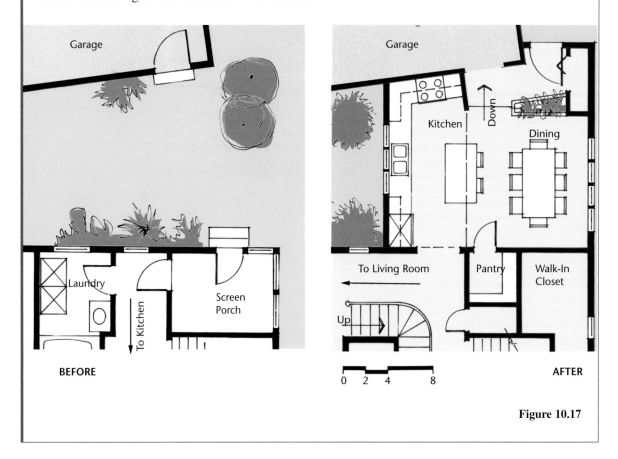

Figure 10.17

PART THREE – THE INTERIOR

CHAPTER 11: Interior Walls and Ceilings

The walls and ceilings of your projects are what the client sees, so you will naturally want to select the finish materials and colors with care and skill. However what lies below the finish surface is just as important—even more so in kitchens and baths, which have to stand up to high moisture, heat and continual use. In this chapter, we'll look at the underlying construction of walls and ceilings to better equip you to design them.

NEW PARTITIONS

We take the interior partitions of our homes for granted but they are there for several reasons. Just think of the many functions the interior walls in your own house perform:

- Provide acoustic separation between rooms so that sounds from one room are reduced or isolated.

- Provide visual separation between rooms to shut out unwanted light and impart privacy.

- Control access to rooms where security of the contents is desirable.

- Contain water (showers, baths).

- Control airflow between rooms to allow different temperatures and to contain odors.

- Interior partitions become bearing walls when needed to support floors or roofs above.

With such heavy demands on them interior partitions deserve good understanding by you, the designer, if they are to meet these challenges.

Wood Stud Partitions

The vast majority of homes in the U.S. employ a single interior wall system: 2x4 wood studs faced with 1/2-inch (13 mm)-thick drywall. The system consists of a double 2x4 top plate and single bottom plate with studs placed at 16 inches (406 mm) on center. Where possible, wall sections are nailed together using the floor deck as a working surface then tilted up into place and fastened to the abutting partitions. Where space prohibits this approach, the base plate is nailed down and the studs installed one by one.

Wood stud partitions can be tweaked in several ways to suit special needs. If the piping in plumbing walls cannot be contained within a 3 1/2 inch (89 mm) cavity, the cavity can be increased to 5 1/2 inches (140 mm) by using 2x6 studs. Ducts that run in the stud cavity may also require thicker cavities. Interior bearing walls call for a double top plate and properly sized headers to span any openings. Partitions in kitchens and baths require blocking between the studs to support cabinets and fixtures. Blocking is also used to adapt openings in the studs for recessed items, such as medicine cabinets. Finally, if the wall finish is anything but drywall, a substrate material may be needed, such as cementitious backerboard under tile.

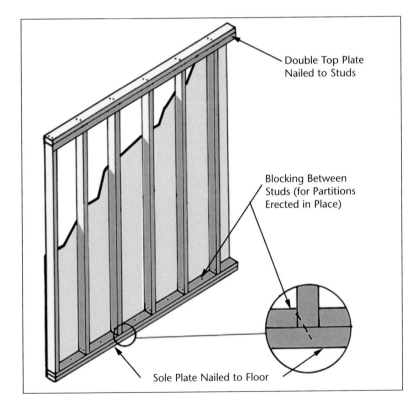

Double Top Plate
Nailed to Studs

Blocking Between
Studs (for Partitions
Erected in Place)

Sole Plate Nailed to Floor

Figure 11.1 A typical interior wood stud partition. If the section can be assembled on the floor then tilted up, the bottom plate can be simply nailed to the studs. Otherwise, the studs are nailed one by one onto the bottom plate, in place, with blocking to keep them in alignment as they are toe nailed into place.

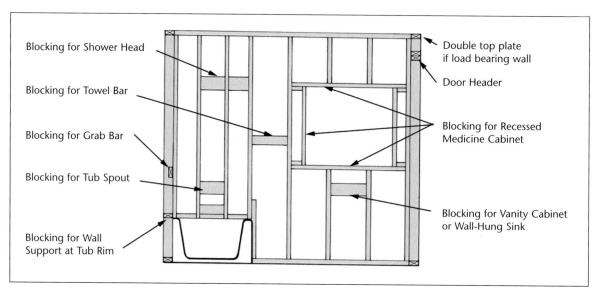

Blocking for Shower Head

Blocking for Towel Bar

Blocking for Grab Bar

Blocking for Tub Spout

Blocking for Wall
Support at Tub Rim

Double top plate
if load bearing wall

Door Header

Blocking for Recessed
Medicine Cabinet

Blocking for Vanity Cabinet
or Wall-Hung Sink

Figure 11.2 Studwalls in bathrooms require additional horizontal blocking to support fixtures, grab bars and openings.

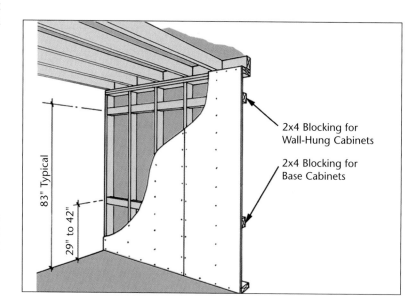

83" Typical

29" to 42"

2x4 Blocking for
Wall-Hung Cabinets

2x4 Blocking for
Base Cabinets

Figure 11.3 New studwalls in kitchens should contain horizontal blocking for attachment of both wall and base cabinets.

Steel Stud Partitions

Steel studs for interior residential partitions are becoming more popular as the quality of wood declines and prices rise. Carpenters who formerly insisted on wood are increasingly willing to learn the sheet metal skills necessary to install steel studs, swayed by the lighter weight, consistency and dependability of the product. Steel studs are cold formed from sheet steel in gauges of 25, 20, 18, 16, 14 and 12 (the lower the number, the heavier the gauge). For typical residential partitions 25-gauge studs work well.

Two types of partition-framing systems are currently in use. The first, evolved from commercial installations, uses a C-shaped track for the top and sole plate, into which the studs are fitted. Studs come in widths of 1 5/8-, 2 1/2-, 3 5/8-, 4- and 6-inches (41 mm, 64 mm, 92 mm, 102 mm, 152 mm), in lengths up to 20 feet (6,096 mm). Installation typically follows a 1-2-3 sequence. The tracks are first screwed to the floor and ceiling structure. Studs are then fitted into the tracks 16- or 24-inches (406 mm or 610 mm) on center and screwed to the tracks. The studs feel flimsy at this point but gain stiffness when the wall finish is screwed to them.

The second system, more adaptable to residential carpentry, is a hybrid of steel and wood. Instead of the C-shaped tracks standard 2x4 wood studs are used. The ends of the steel studs are pre-cut to fit over the 2x4s. These studs measure 3 1/2 inches (89 mm) wide to match wood studs. This allows you to use wood blocking around door openings and recesses.

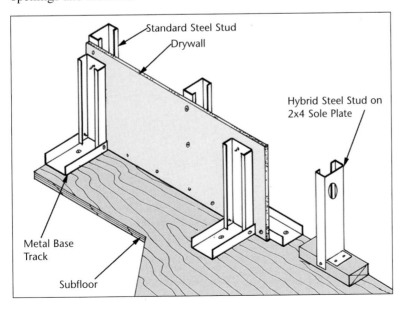

Figure 11.4 Standard steel stud partitions (left) consist of C-shaped studs that nest into C-shaped tracks screwed to the floor and ceiling. A hybrid system (right) comes with ends adapted to fit over 2x4 wood plates.

151

Sound-Dampening Partitions

One of the functions of interior partitions we first mentioned is acoustic privacy. Any parent with teenagers in the household probably understands the need for isolating the transmission of sound within the house. Sound transmission can also be a concern in rooms adjacent to bathrooms, which are exposed to the noise of running water and flushing toilets. Masonry walls have enough mass to make them naturally resistant to sound transmission but are not practical options in light-framed homes. Standard wood or steel stud partitions clad with drywall do little to shield one room from noise in the next one.

Sound transmission through walls is measured in STC units (sound transmission classification). How various STC ratings affect what you can hear on the other side of the wall are listed below:

STC Rating	Sound Transmission
25	Normal speech can easily be understood
30	Loud speech can be understood
35	Loud speech heard but not understood
42	Loud speech audible as a murmur
45	Must strain to hear loud speech
48	Some loud speech barely audible
50	Loud speech not audible

Data obtained from NAHB and other sources

Figure 11.5 shows several ways to improve the sound resistance of studwalls for both existing and new partitions. Each method cuts sound transmission by either adding mass, adding sound-dampening insulation, isolating one wall surface from the others, or a combination of these. Since sound also travels through openings in ducts and door cracks, it is probably not cost effective to try to achieve an STC of greater than 50 without also isolating the ductwork and installing gaskets around the doors and this is somewhat unusual in an interior door.

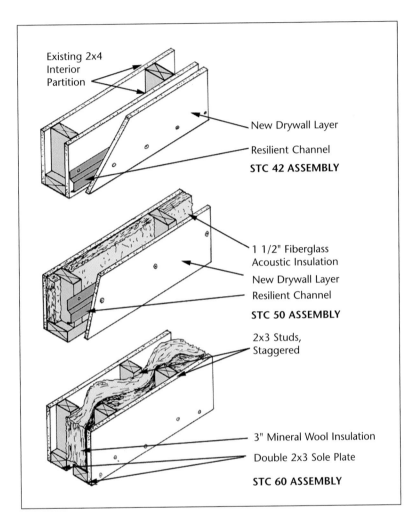

Existing 2x4
Interior
Partition

New Drywall Layer

Resilient Channel

STC 42 ASSEMBLY

1 1/2" Fiberglass
Acoustic Insulation

New Drywall Layer

Resilient Channel

STC 50 ASSEMBLY

2x3 Studs,
Staggered

3" Mineral Wool Insulation

Double 2x3 Sole Plate

STC 60 ASSEMBLY

Figure 11.5 Three ways to increase the sound-dampening capability of a typical studwall.

SPECIAL FRAMING

It would be unusual for a home requiring the services of a kitchen/bath designer to consist of nothing beyond straight, unbroken, interior partitions. Curved walls, surrounds for bath fixtures and arched openings are some of the ingredients that you should have on your design palette. While you won't need to know exactly how to frame these items, you should have a general idea of their construction to help you know what is feasible and what to include in your drawings and specifications.

Enclosing Tubs and Spas

The three-fixture, 5-foot x 7-foot (1,524 mm x 2,134 mm) bathroom is no longer the standard. Today's baths tend to be larger and likely feature a more diversified layout. Also, there is more choice in fixtures. Some of these fixtures, such as pedestal sinks and claw-foot bathtubs, simply stand free in an open space. Others, such as toilets, tubs and whirlpools are designed to fit into site-built enclosures that may be straight or curved. These enclosures are made up of stick framing of the same general type used for interior partitions with added provisions for attached items and finishes. When laying out the design, check the manufacturer's rough-in dimensions of the fixture so you can allow enough clearance for both the fixture and wall finish above the fixture. Fully recessed bathtubs or whirlpools require support by a single or double cripple wall framed with 2x4s. Specify proper blocking to support the bottom of the unit per the manufacturer's data.

Whirlpools are usually larger and hold more water than bathtubs and come with equipment that heats and circulates the water. These differences make the enclosure for a whirlpool more complicated than for a bathtub. In a renovation first consider how the tub unit can be moved into place. Doorways and stairs in an existing house may not be wide enough for a large unit, which may have to be moved in through a nearby window or opening created in the wall. Next, check out the weight of the unit when full and make sure the floor structure below the installation site is capable of supporting the weight. The supporting platform can consist of a single- or double-width cripple wall. Users can step over a single wall, but must sit on the platform created by a double wall and swing their legs over into the bathtub. Be sure to specify the location of the access panel for the pump at the plumbing end. Also pin down the location of any blocking required in the surrounding walls for grab bars or other items to be mounted to the walls. Consider specifying insulation around the platform walls both to help control noise and to keep the water warm.

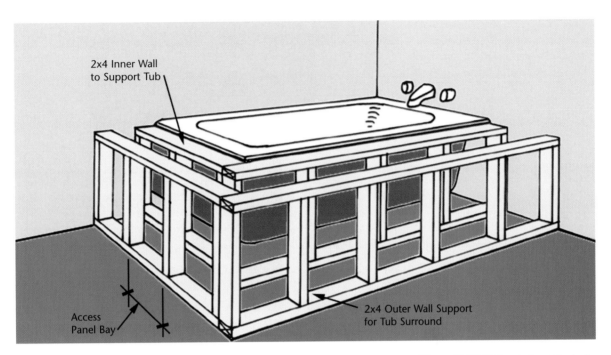

2x4 Inner Wall
to Support Tub

Access
Panel Bay

2x4 Outer Wall Support
for Tub Surround

Figure 11.6 Whirlpools (spas) typically sit on single or double kneewalls. Always provide for access to the pump.

Shower Enclosures

Showers today are just as likely to be separate as combined with the tub. Separate showers are enclosed in several ways, depending on the type of fixture. A site-built shower with tiled floor and walls can fit any wall configuration. The enclosing walls are framed with studs similar to other interior partitions with solid 2-by blocking installed to support the shower head and any grab bars or other items to be attached to the walls. The floor is tiled, as described in the following chapter.

A second type of shower is shipped as a one-piece unit, with ceiling, walls and floor formed seamlessly out of acrylic or fiberglass-reinforced polyester (Figure 11.7). It simply mounts into a stud surround built to the specified rough opening dimensions.

There's also a hybrid approach consisting of site-built walls with a prefabricated one-piece plastic base (Figure 11.8). Several base sizes and shapes are available for fully recessed or corner installations. However, the enclosing walls must follow the shape of the base faithfully. The rough opening dimensions of the base determines the position of the studs.

Figure 11.7 A one-piece shower unit must be positioned before the framing enclosure, which consists of studs and blocking as required by the manufacturer.

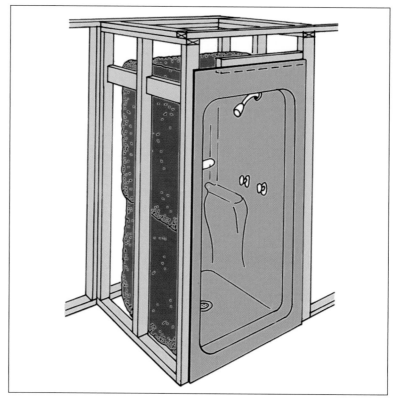

Figure 11.8 A site-built shower can be built on a tiled base or prefabricated base. Prefab bases are available for one-, two-, or three-wall showers in various sizes.

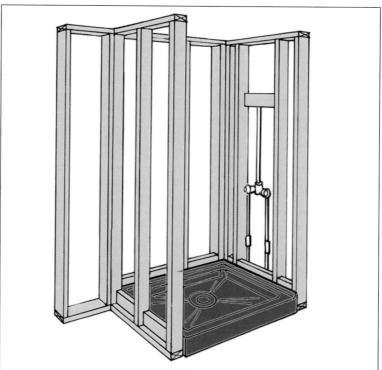

Curved Surfaces

Another trend in home design is an increased use of curved walls. Framing a curved wall is similar to framing a rectilinear wall, except that the top and sole plates must take the shape of the curve. Plates can be made up of two layers of plywood or can consist of metal assemblies specifically made for this purpose. Any material that can be bent into a curve can be used for the finish. A common choice is two layers of 3/8 inch (10 mm) drywall, installed after wetting the top (outward-facing) surface.

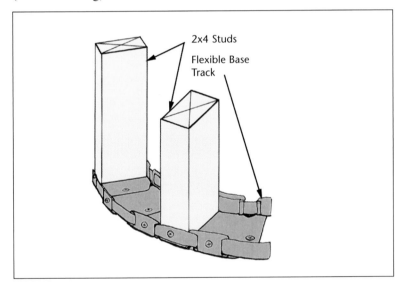

Figure 11.9 An adjustable metal floor and ceiling track is available for curved walls. The track is simply nailed to the floor and ceiling in the desired shape, then the studs are installed.

Along with curved walls, arched passageways add elegance and interest to many of today's kitchen and bath designs. There are three types of common arch shapes: Roman (half-circle), segmental and elliptical. The arc of an arch begins at a spring line, the horizontal line extending between supports. Roman arches rise highest above the spring line, making them impractical for wide openings in rooms with standard height ceilings. Segmented arches are flatter with less rise, but have sharp corners at the spring points. Elliptical arches can rise as much as desired and meet the spring line at a flatter curve.

All arches are framed below a straight top plate and header and the header must carry any load above, if the wall is a bearing wall. The arch can be framed with sides cut to the shape of the arch and 2x4 spacers set between the sides along the bottom of the arch, as shown in Figure 11.11. The sides can be made of 1x pine if the arch height is less than 11 inches (279 mm), or 3/4-inch (19 mm) thick plywood, for higher arches. Special PVC and metal corner beads are available to fit around a curve, for plaster or drywall wall finish.

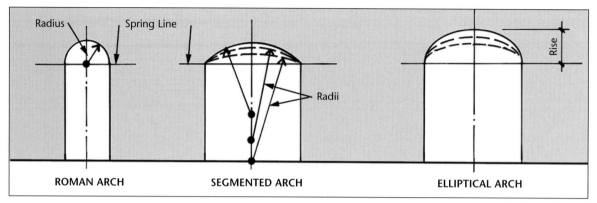

ROMAN ARCH   SEGMENTED ARCH   ELLIPTICAL ARCH

Figure 11.10 Roman arches are half-circles with the center point along the spring line. The center point for segmented arches lies below the spring line—the lower the point, the flatter the arch. Elliptical arches can also be flat or rise as high as desired.

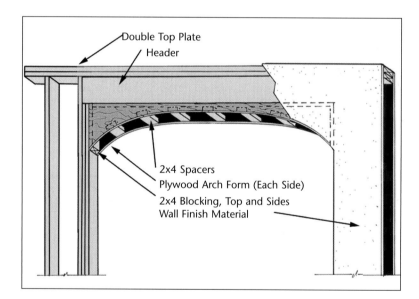

Figure 11.11 Frame an arch into an opening under a header using plywood sides and 2x4 spacers.

Accommodating Recessed Items

Medicine cabinets, toilet paper holders and other items recessed into the wall require a rough opening with framing on all sides. Most medicine cabinets are available in depths that allow them to fit into a standard 3 1/2 inch (89 mm) stud cavity, but they take up the entire cavity, with nothing except the wall finish of the adjacent room on the backside. This creates a sound path that can be a problem in some cases. If the medicine cabinet backs up to a bedroom, for example, any sounds in the bath will be heard easily in the bedroom. Possible solutions include substituting a surface-mounted cabinet or relocating the recessed cabinet to another wall, such as one backing into a closet.

CEILING STRUCTURES

The ceiling of a room may simply be a finish material attached to the underside of the floor or roof structure above it or a separate structure built below it. The high ceilings found in many old houses may be an asset in large rooms but make small rooms seem even smaller. A new ceiling at a lower height can make the room feel wider. It might also provide a needed chase in which to enclose mechanical or electrical systems. Codes allow ceiling heights in kitchens and baths to be as low as 7 feet (2,134 mm). There are two main ways to support a separate ceiling:

- Metal or wood joists attached to the walls

- Metal grids suspended from the structure above

Wall-Hung Ceilings

Framing for this type begins with ledgers attached to opposite walls on the long sides of the room. Joists are then attached to the ledgers with metal joist hangers. Since the ceiling supports no load other than its own, the joists can be sized accordingly. And if the ceiling finish material is drywall that does not have to carry the weight of insulation, it can be 1/2-inch thick. The table, "Joists for Lowered Ceilings," can guide you in sizing ceiling joists.

Joists for Lowered Ceilings (Joists assumed to carry weight of ceiling materials only plus 10 lb. live load)		
Span	**Joist Size and Spacing Options**	
Up to 8 feet (2,438 mm)	2x4 @ 24" (610 mm) o.c.	
Up to 10 feet (3,048 mm)	2x4 @ 16" (406 mm) o.c.	2x6 @ 24" (610 mm) o.c.
10 to 14 feet (3,048 to 4,267 mm)	2x6 @ 16" (406 mm) o.c.	2x8 @ 24" (610 mm) o.c.
14 to 18 feet (4,267 mm to 5,486 mm)	2x8 @ 16" (406 mm) o.c.	2x10 @ 24" (610 mm) o.c.

Adapted from data published by the Southern Pine Marketing Council

Suspended Ceilings

The lightweight suspended ceilings that have long been the standard in non-residential buildings are sometimes used in homes. The most common type consists of a light-gauge metal grid hung by wires from the structure above. The finish material is most often acoustical tiles that fit into the tee-shaped members of the grid, which gives it its tag, "lay-in ceiling." Fluorescent lighting fixtures are also available in sizes to fit into a lay-in grid. While this system is fast and economical, it creates an ambiance similar to an office building, so think twice before specifying it for a home.

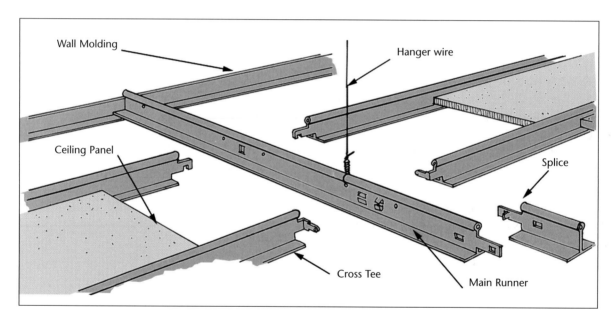

Figure 11.12 Lay-in ceilings consist of a metal grid suspended by wires from the structure above and modular panels that "lay" into the grid.

Another type of lightweight metal suspension ceiling is better suited to the type of finishes associated with homes. A "**hat-channel ceiling**," also consists of a metal grid, but one to which standard residential finishes can attach. The main grid members are C-shaped channels which support secondary channels that resemble an inverted hat. Drywall can then be screwed to the hat channels.

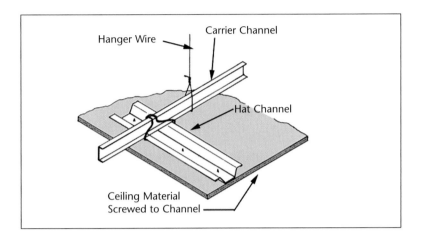

Figure 11.13 An indirect-hung metal ceiling is constructed by hanging metal carrier channels from the structure above, then wiring hat channels to the carrier channels. A ceiling finish material, such as drywall, can then be screwed to the hat channels.

Soffits

You may find it advantageous to drop portions of ceilings, rather than just running them into the side walls. For example the space between the top of kitchen wall cabinets and the ceiling, left open, just collects dust and wastes potentially valuable space. Cabinets that extend fully to the ceiling put this space to use, creating storage space for infrequently used items such as punch bowls and party accessories. Alternatively, the space can be closed off with a soffit, or "bulkhead," flush with the face of the cabinets or extending outward to contain lighting for the countertops below, as shown in Figure 11.14. In a large bathroom, a dropped soffit over certain fixtures, such as a whirlpool, can help define these areas and make the room more interesting.

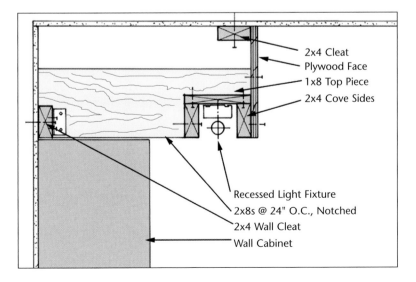

Figure 11.14 Extend a soffit out to align with the front of the base cabinet to create a location for task lighting above the countertop.

MODIFYING EXISTING WALLS AND CEILINGS

Any redesign to an existing kitchen or bath will likely entail changes to the wall or ceiling surfaces for any of several reasons:

- The wall may need to be removed completely to suit the new design.

- The condition of the existing substrate or finish is too poor to apply a new finish directly.

- A chase is needed to house pipes or wiring.

- The substrate is too uneven or out of plumb for installation of new cabinetry or fixtures.

- Insulation and/or a vapor barrier must be added to upgrade an outside wall.

- A new opening is required in a bearing wall.

You can assess most wall conditions by just looking at them with an eye out for crumbling plaster, dampness and cracks. Check the straightness of the walls by holding a long straight-edge both vertically and horizontally along the length of the wall. When any of the above-mentioned conditions occur on interior partitions, the quickest and easiest solution might be to demolish the partition and replace it with a new one. But don't specify removal of any bearing walls unless alternative support is provided. And it may only be necessary to gut one side of a partition, leaving the structure and other side intact.

Modifying Bearing Walls

Partitions that merely separate interior spaces support no structural load imposed from above and can thus be removed or altered without consequence. But bearing wall partitions that support another floor, ceiling or roof should not be cut into before you provide an alternate means of transferring the loads down through the structure. The first task, of course, is to be sure that it is a bearing wall. Here are some general clues for spotting interior bearing walls:

- A partition that runs along the long direction of the floor plan, near the center is likely a bearing wall.

- If the beam line in the basement has a wall situated above it on the first floor, it is likely a bearing wall.

- If there is an attic above the partition in question, inspect the area above the partition to see if joists overlap near the partition. If so, you can assume the partition carries them.

If you can't determine the structural status of a partition, obtain the advice of an architect or structural engineer before proceeding with your design. Some interior walls in earthquake-prone and high-wind regions are reinforced to counter horizontal (shear) forces. Shear walls can usually be spotted by the way they are built. An interior shear wall would typically be clad in OSB or plywood or reinforced along the diagonals with metal or wood bracing. When altering shear walls, you have to provide alternate means for transferring the shear stresses and should consult an architect or structural engineer. Interior bearing walls should be temporarily shored on both sides before their structural components are dismantled. Be sure to specify that the shoring start at the ground and extend to the floor or ceiling structure above the walls to be removed.

Any new openings in bearing walls require appropriately sized header beams. The table, "Headers for Interior Bearing Walls," gives the required header beam sizes for partitions that support a floor or roof above. If the partition supports only an attic floor, the sizes of the table are conservative. If the partition supports more than one floor, the headers are undersized and you should consult a building design professional for help in sizing a header. Doubled headers are given in the table except for spans over 8 feet (2,438 mm), which requires three 2x12s. Because you can't fit three 2-bys into a 2x4 stud wall you should consider using an LVL header. Provide solid bearing under the ends of each header beam, equivalent to at least one 2x4 trimmer stud.

HEADERS FOR INTERIOR BEARING WALLS		
Clear Width of Opening in Interior Partition	**Header Size**	
	Yard Lumber	Laminated Veneer Lumber
3 feet (914 mm) or less	Two 2x8s	One LVL 1 3/4 x 5 1/2 (44 mm x 140 mm)
4 to 5 feet (1,219 mm to 1,524 mm)	Two 2x10s	One LVL 1 3/4 x 5 1/2 (44 mm x 140 mm)
5 to 7 feet (1,524 mm to 2,134 mm)	Two 2x12s	Two LVL 1 3/4 x 5 1/2 (44 mm x 140 mm)
7 to 8 feet (2,134 mm to 2,438 mm)	Two 2x12s	Two LVL 1 3/4 x 7 1/4 (44 mm x 184 mm)
8 to 9 feet (2,438 mm to 2,743 mm)	Three 2x12s	Two LVL 1 3/4 x 7 1/4 (44 mm x 184 mm)

The assumed bending stress of the lumber (Fb) is 900 psi. The load width assumed is 12 feet (3,658 mm), typical for a bearing wall that runs down the middle of a 24-foot (7,315 mm)-wide house.

Furring Walls or Ceilings

If an existing surface is too uneven to accept a new finish or the studs are irregularly spaced, you can make the surface even by attaching furring strips (strapping) across the framing. Furring strips also provide supports for equipment or cabinets and the space between the furring and old wall can contain pipes, wires or insulation, providing the proper protection is placed over them to prevent puncturing from nails or screws.

The furring material can be standard 1x3 wood furring strips, if nothing more than a nail-base substrate is the goal. Furring strips are thick enough to hold screws but too thin to even out an uneven wall unless shims are inserted at the hollow portions of the wall. Some installers prefer to avoid shimming by using stiffer furring made from 2x3s or 2x4s. Another reason for using 2x furring is that when new wiring must be run through the gap created by the furring, it must be held at least 1 1/4 inches (32 mm) back from the face of the framing to meet the electrical code and to prevent puncturing by nails. This requirement can be met by having the cable stapled to the existing wall surface. Of course, if the old wall/ceiling finish is stripped off, the wiring can simply run in the wall cavity.

Figure 11.15 Existing walls must often be furred (strapped) out for a variety of reasons. The method shown here entails stripping off the old wall finish and attaching furring strips to the framing. Shims between the furring and studs can adjust for out-of-plumb or irregular studs.

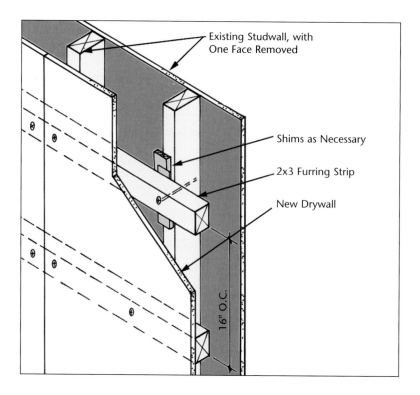

Existing Studwall, with
One Face Removed

Shims as Necessary

2x3 Furring Strip

New Drywall

16" O.C.

Sistering Studs

Just as adding a new "sister" joist to the side of an existing one can level an uneven floor (See Chapter 7) a sister stud can be added to even out a wall or increase its thickness once the old finish has been stripped off. Before you specify this method, however, make sure the existing studs are spaced close enough together to provide a sound support for the wall finish material. If they are too far apart, you'll probably be better off furring the wall with strips applied horizontally over the old studs, as described on page 164.

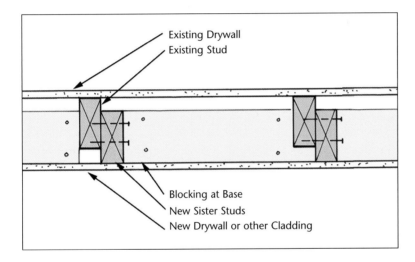

Existing Drywall
Existing Stud

Blocking at Base
New Sister Studs
New Drywall or other Cladding

Figure 11.16 Sistering studs onto the existing studs may be required to widen the wall for piping or additional insulation.

CASE STUDY #5 – IMPROVING A KITCHEN LAYOUT

The location of interior walls can mean the difference between a plan that comes up short and one that works. The wall separating the kitchen from the dining room in this North Carolina house underscored the narrow, cramped feel of the kitchen. The door between the two rooms isolated the kitchen even more. Lack of preparation space was another problem in the kitchen. All of these deficiencies were overcome with a scheme that called for removing the wall between kitchen and dining room and installing a countertop that does double duty as a breakfast bar and preparation surface. The former dining niche became a site for a base cabinet containing the sink, which overlooks the backyard through a bank of casement windows. Relocating the doorway to the hall created a corner niche for the refrigerator.

Because the wall to be demolished was a bearing wall it couldn't be removed without providing alternative support for the roof above. This was accomplished with an adequately sized beam above the new opening. The changes make the kitchen function better and feel much larger.

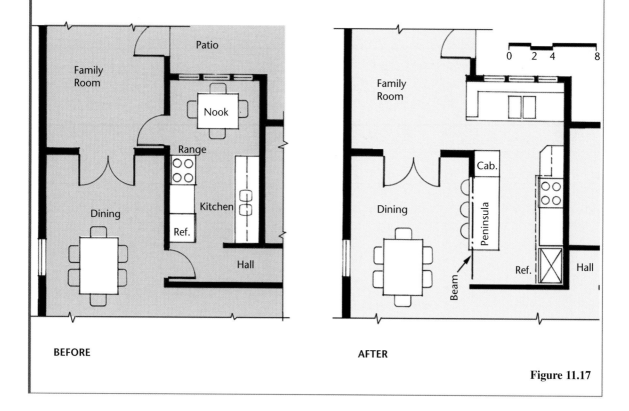

BEFORE

AFTER

Figure 11.17

CHAPTER 12: Interior Surfaces

The surfaces of the floors, walls, ceilings and cabinets may not be the most important part of your project, but they are what your client sees and will have intimate contact with after the project is completed. If you want satisfied clients, you must understand the various kinds of finishes available then guide your clients through the decision-making process. This will require an open attitude and ability to communicate the pros and cons of the many options. Also expect to spend some time helping your client sort through a pile of product information, samples, pictures and cost data. If you do this well, you'll create an appealing interior and leave the project with a happy customer.

THE SURFACE BENEATH THE SURFACE

The statement "beauty is more than skin deep" is never truer than with the finishes of a room. Too often homeowners paint or paper over an old wall or ceiling to find that the new finish reveals all of the imperfections of the old one. Or, a short time later, the finish chips or flakes off because of the poor condition of the substrate. The proper substrate is crucial, particularly in kitchens and baths, where moisture is always a factor. Thin finishes such as wallcoverings require smooth, even substrates to which they can adhere. Paint is likely the least forgiving finish, most demanding of a well-prepared substrate. In the following sections, we'll look at some floor, wall and ceiling substrates, with an eye toward selecting them for the desired finish material. Then we'll see how to apply new substrates to existing surfaces in remodeling jobs.

Plaster

The wall and ceiling substrate of most homes built before the 1940s consisted of thin strips of wood lath over which plaster was applied. The process was time consuming and labor intensive but nevertheless resulted in a sound, perfectly smooth surface capable of accepting paint or wallpaper, though the latter was most often the finish of choice. The main ingredient of traditional plaster was quicklime, crushed limestone heated to a high temperature. Before mixing with water into a form usable for construction, water was added to the lime powder, which was then left to hydrate (slake) for three weeks on site. The resulting butter-like paste was then mixed with sand and water to create plaster that was troweled on in three separate layers: a rough coat, a brown (scratch) coat and a finish coat. Each layer used a finer grade of sand. Animal hair mixed into the first two coats bound the material together. Rough-sawn wood lath, nailed to the studs with gaps between each lath strip, provided the support for the plaster. Expanded metal lath was used to bend around corners and arches.

Homeowners today who want the best still prefer plaster and are increasingly willing to pay for it, but the material is now applied in different ways than in former times. There are three techniques in use today:

1. Plaster on metal lath

2. Plaster on gypsum lath

3. Skim-coat plaster on blueboard

Plaster on metal lath. Expanded metal lath looks like wire mesh. When stapled to the studs, it provides a stable backing that can be bent around corners or curves. A skilled applicator can trowel on plaster to create a smooth surface on even the most difficult curves. Metal lath requires three coats of plaster, similar to the process with traditional wood lath, making it the most solid, if most expensive way, to plaster a wall or ceiling.

Plaster on gypsum lath. For applications with only straight walls, plaster can be troweled onto panels of gypsum lath, which contains a gypsum core faced with a multi-layer paper formulated for good adhesion to troweled-on plaster. Gypsum lath panels are 1/2 inch (13 mm) or 3/8 inch (10 mm) thick, 16 inches (406 mm) wide and 48 inches or 96 inches (1,219 mm or 2,438 mm) long. They are screwed or nailed across the studs.

Skim-coat plaster on blueboard. A process that has emerged in the last two decades has mostly replaced traditional plastering in residential walls and ceilings. Also known as "veneer plastering," skim-coat is a thin layer of plaster applied over a special gypsum panel called blueboard. Done professionally, the process attains a plaster-like quality at far less cost than either of the prior techniques. The process costs more than the more standard drywall but has several advantages. The coating covers the entire surface, leaving no unevenness between the joints of the drywall and center field. There is also better sound dampening, better fire resistance, no sanding and the surface can be painted within 24 hours of the skim-coat application.

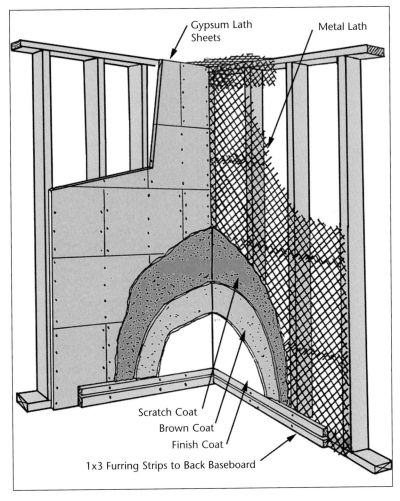

Gypsum Lath
Sheets

Metal Lath

Scratch Coat
Brown Coat
Finish Coat
1x3 Furring Strips to Back Baseboard

Figure 12.1 Finishing walls with traditional plaster begins with nailing a gypsum lath or metal lath substrate to the studs, then applying the plaster in a three-coat process.

Drywall

Today's most familiar wall substrate is known by several names: drywall, gypsum drywall, gyp-board and gypsum wallboard. You are more apt to recognize it by the trade name of the most dominant brand, Sheetrock®. The material arose out of the necessity to build a lot of houses quickly at the end of World War II. It became an instant hit, replacing traditional plaster almost overnight and for good reasons. It came in modular panels 4-feet wide by 8-feet tall, just tall enough for a ceiling in the post-war housing standard. Panels could be easily cut by scoring one side with a knife, snapping the joint in two and cutting the backside. Installation required much less skill than plaster. Panels were quickly nailed to the studs, then finished by applying paper tape to the joints with a plaster-based paste. The joints were sanded smooth, yielding a completely flat and even substrate for wall finishes such as paint or wallpaper.

Drywall is a fairly simple sandwich of a gypsum plaster core faced with paper on each side. The core and facing paper can be varied to produce specific products to suit various applications. Four types are in common use in homes:

- Standard wallboard, for walls in dry areas, with a light gray paper that accepts paint and wallpaper.

- Water-resisting (WR) wallboard (greenboard), containing an impregnated core and water-resistant facing for use as a base for ceramic tile and other non-absorbent finish materials in wet areas. Generally considered acceptable for kitchen and bath surfaces occasionally, but not continuously exposed to water.

- Blueboard, intended for skim-coat plaster finish or tile applied with thinset or elastomeric compounds, but not suitable for inside showers or above tubs.

- Fire Code (Type-X) is used on walls or ceiling surfaces that separate an enclosed garage from living spaces, where the code requires a fire-rated separation.

Drywall panels today come in 4-foot (1,219 mm) widths, in lengths of 8, 10 and 12 feet (2,438 mm, 3,048 mm, 3,658 mm). The 1/2 inch (13 mm) thickness is most common in residential walls and ceilings, but 5/8 inch (16-mm)-thick drywall is preferred in quality construction for walls, particularly where an absolutely flat, solid surface is desired (though this is overkill for a skim-coat plaster finish). Curved walls can be created using two layers of 1/4-inch (6-mm)-thick drywall.

A panoply of plastic and metal accessories stand ready to trim corners and create special surface shapes. The standard metal corner bead that turns a sharp corner has been augmented by PVC in 90-degree and rounded (bullnose) shapes.

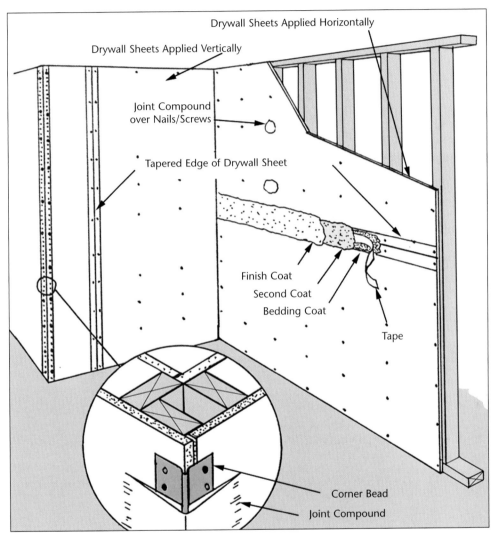

Drywall Sheets Applied Horizontally

Drywall Sheets Applied Vertically

Joint Compound over Nails/Screws

Tapered Edge of Drywall Sheet

Finish Coat

Second Coat

Bedding Coat

Tape

Corner Bead

Joint Compound

Figure 12.2 Drywall panels can install vertically or horizontally. Joints are taped with paper or fiberglass imbedded in drywall compound and more compound is used over screws and nails. A variety of metal and plastic trim pieces are now available to trim corners (inset).

171

Backerboards

Figure 12.3 Cementitious backerboard is the preferred substrate for tile in wet areas. Cut the panels by scoring or cutting with a carbide-tipped saw blade, then nailing or screwing into place with CBU nails. Joints must be taped with open mesh fiberglass tape. Thinsetting compound bonds the tile to the backerboard.

As mentioned on page 170, greenboard drywall is specially formulated to resist water as a tile backer material. However, while it provides an acceptable substrate for tile in basically dry areas, such as kitchen or bathroom walls, it does not resist water in wet areas such as above tubs or inside showers as dependably as two more-recent materials. One is **cement board**, as mentioned in Chapter 8 as an underlayment for tile floors, another is **gypsum backerboard**, a newer material with a gypsum core reinforced with fiberglass mats and faced with a water-resistant paper.

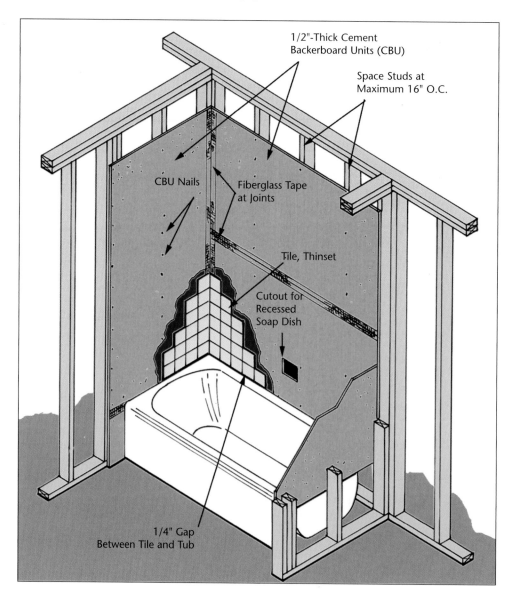

1/2"-Thick Cement Backerboard Units (CBU)

Space Studs at Maximum 16" O.C.

CBU Nails

Fiberglass Tape at Joints

Tile, Thinset

Cutout for Recessed Soap Dish

1/4" Gap Between Tile and Tub

Plywood

We learned of the use of plywood as a structural wall and roof sheathing in prior chapters. This versatile product also makes an excellent substrate for certain floor and countertop finishes. Plywood can do double duty as both subfloor and substrate for most hardwood flooring and carpeting. If filled and sanded, it also works for sheet floorcoverings or vinyl tiles, but it is usually easier and less costly to apply an underlayment of 1/4-inch-thick Luan (a type of mahogany) plywood underlayment for these floorcoverings. Plywood can back ceramic tiles on floors or countertops if the smoothed-face plywood bearing the correct grade is specified. Call for exterior grade, exposure 1, which appears on the grade stamp as "A-C GROUP 1, EXTERIOR," where the "A" surface has been plugged and smoothed and the "Exterior" label indicates that water-resistant glues have been used.

Plywood grading can be confusing. In general, plywood is graded according to the appearance of the facing veneer, strength characteristics and water resistance. The plywood industry uses six letters to code the surface appearance.

N – Smooth surface "natural finish" veneer is select, all heartwood or all sapwood, free of open defects with a maximum of six repairs per 4x8 panel, made parallel to the grain and well matched for the grain and color.

A – This smooth, paintable veneer allows not more than 18 neatly made repairs, boat, sled or router type and parallel to the grain. It may be used as natural finish in less demanding applications.

B – Solid-surface veneer permits shims, circular repair plugs, tight knots to 1 inch across the grain and minor splits.

C – This veneer has tight knots to 1 1/2 inches. It has knotholes to 1 inch across the grain with some to 1 1/2 inches if the total width of knots and knotholes is within specified limits. Repairs are synthetic or wood. Discoloration and sanding defects that do not impair strength are permitted. Limited splits and stitching are allowed.

D – Knots and knotholes to 2 1/2 inches in width across the grain and 1/2 inch larger within specified limits, are allowed. Limited splits are permitted. This face grade is limited to interior (exposure 1 or 2) panels.

The tables here list some of the American Plywood Association (APA) grades for some grades of plywood you are most likely to encounter in kitchen and bath applications.

EXTERIOR PANELS		
APA Grade	Available Thicknesses, inches (mm)	Grade Designation, Description, and Uses
APA RATED SHEATHING STRUCTURAL 1 EXTERIOR	5/16 (8 mm) 3/8 (10 mm) 1/2 (13 mm) 5/8 (16 mm) 3/4 (19 mm)	**APA Structural 1 & 2 Rated Sheathing EXT** For engineered applications in construction and industry where resistance to permanent exposure to weather or moisture is required; manufactured as conventional veneered plywood, as a composite, or as a nonveneered panel; unsanded structural 1 more commonly available.
APA RATED STURD-I-FLOOR EXTERIOR	5/8 (16 mm) 3/4 (19 mm)	**APA Rated Sturd-I-Floor EXT** For combination subfloor-underlayment under carpet where severe moisture conditions may be present, as in balcony decks, high concentrated and impact load resistance; manufactured as conventional veneered plywood, as a composite, or as a nonveneered panel; available square-edge or tongue-and-groove.
APA A-C EXTERIOR	1/2 (13 mm)	**APA A-C Ext** For use where appearance of only one side is important: soffits, fences, structural uses.
APA UNDERLAYMENT C-C PLUGGED EXTERIOR	3/8 (10 mm) 1/2 (13 mm) 5/8 (16 mm) 3/4 (19 mm)	**APA UNDERLAYMENT C-C PLUGGED EXT** For application over structural subfloor; smooth surface for application of carpet and high concentrated and impact load resistance; touch-sanded; for areas to be covered with thin resilient flooring (using panels with sanded face).

INTERIOR PANELS		
APA Grade	**Available Thicknesses, inches (mm)**	**Grade Designation, Description, and Uses**
APA RATED SHEATHING EXPOSURE 1	5/16 (8 mm) 3/8 (10 mm) 1/2 (13 mm) 5/8 (16 mm) 3/4 (19 mm)	**APA Rated Sheathing Exp 1 or 2** Specially designed for subflooring and wall and roof sheathing, but also used for a broad arrange of other applications; manufactured as conventional veneered plywood, as a composite, or as a nonveneered panel; exposure 1.
APA RATED STURD-I-FLOOR EXPOSURE 1	5/8 (16 mm) 3/4 (19 mm)	**APA Rated Sturd-I-Floor Exp 1 or 2** Specifically designed as a combination subfloor-underlayment; smooth surface for application of carpet and high concentrated and impact load resistance; manufactured as conventional veneered plywood, as a composite, or as a reconstituted wood panel (waferboard, oriented strand-board, structural particleboard); available square-edge or tongue-and-groove.
APA UNDERLAYMENT C-C PLUGGED EXTERIOR	3/8 (10 mm) 1/2 (13 mm) 5/8 (16 mm) 3/4 (19 mm)	**APA UNDERLAYMENT C-C PLUGGED EXT** For application over structural subfloor; smooth surface for application of carpet and high concentrated and impact load resistance; touch-sanded; for areas to be covered with thin resilient flooring (using panels with sanded face).
APA UNDERLAYMENT GROUP 1 INTERIOR	3/8 (10 mm) 1/2 (13 mm) 5/8 (16 mm) 3/4 (19 mm)	**APA UNDERLAYMENT INT** For application over structural subfloor; smooth surface for application of carpet and high concentrated and impact load resistance; touch-sanded; for areas to be covered with thin resilient flooring (using panels with sanded face).
APA A-D GROUP 1 INTERIOR	1/4 (6 mm) 3/8 (10 mm) 1/2 (13 mm) 5/8 (16 mm) 3/4 (19 mm)	**APA A-D INT** For use where appearance of only one side is important; paneling, built-ins, shelving, and partitions.
APA B-D GROUP-2 INTERIOR	1/4 (6 mm) 3/8 (10 mm) 1/2 (13 mm) 5/8 (16 mm) 3/4 (19 mm)	**APA B-D INT** Utility panel with one solid side; good for backing, sides of built-ins, shelving, etc.

Concrete and Concrete Block

Cementitious materials work fairly well as a substrate for ceramic tile. Both concrete and concrete block can back plaster. If a wallcovering is the desired finish, a skim coat of plaster must be applied to yield a substrate that is smooth enough for the wallcovering. Another way to apply a finish other than paint to a masonry wall is to fur it out first, then attach drywall to the furring (strapping).

The following table summarizes what we've learned about substrates and tells what must be done to each to provide an acceptable base for various wall or ceiling finishes.

	SUITABLE WALL OR CEILING SUBSTRATE		
Substrates	**Proposed Wall or Ceiling Finish**		
	Paint	Wallcovering	Ceramic Tile
New plaster	Acceptable, if primed	Acceptable	Acceptable in dry areas
Drywall	Acceptable if joints taped and sanded smooth and primed	Acceptable if joints taped and sanded smooth	Blueboard in walls/ceilings only occasionally wet.
Old wallpaper, sound condition	Acceptable if sealed with shellac or oil-based primer	Acceptable if old wallpaper is sound and sealed	Not acceptable
Old wallpaper, poor condition	Strip paper and patch wall beneath or apply new substrate	Strip paper and patch wall beneath or apply new substrate	Not acceptable
Old vinyl wallcovering, sound condition	Seal first with shellac or oil-based primer	Seal first with shellac or oil-based primer	Not acceptable
Old vinyl wallcovering, poor condition	Strip wallcovering and patch wall beneath or apply new substrate	Strip wallcovering and patch wall beneath or apply new substrate	Not acceptable
Cement or gypsum backerboard	Not acceptable	Not acceptable	Acceptable
Plywood, filled and sanded	Not acceptable	Acceptable	Acceptable except in showers and around tubs
Concrete or concrete block	Acceptable if dry and rustic effect desired	Not acceptable	Acceptable if smoothed and filled or mortar set

FLOOR FINISH MATERIALS

You have a wider variety of floor finishes for your design palette than ever before. However, the success of the finish you specify depends on a sound floor structure, the proper substrate, provisions for moisture control and attention to the specific installation requirements of the finish. And don't lose track of the functions these finishes must fulfill. When bath floors get wet, they get slick and become hazardous, so it doesn't make sense to specify one that is slick to begin with. Below we explore some of the most popular kitchen and bath floor finishes and some of the things you should know to specify them effectively.

Ceramic Tile, Cement Tile and Stone

The variety of tiles made from mineral sources abounds in color, pattern and size. All are porous, brittle and usually installed by tile or masonry contractors. **Ceramic tiles** are made of various colors of clay, fused into a solid under high temperatures in a kiln. Unglazed tiles are preferred for floors because of their better traction—an especially important feature in baths. **Cement tiles** are made in much the same way as concrete, by combining Portland cement with water and a fine aggregate. **Stone tiles** of granite, shale, bluestone and other species, are increasing in popularity. Several types of **manufactured tiles** augment the list. Most all mineral-based tiles install on floors in one of two basic methods:

- Thinsetting them into a special thinset mortar compound troweled over the subfloor or concrete slab

- Mudsetting them into a mortar bed

Thinsetting works well for all but shower floors, which must be sloped for drainage. The best solution for shower floors is to set them in a full mortar bed. The mortar bed slopes a minimum of 1/4 inch per foot toward the drain, which usually requires a mortar bed thickness that varies from 1 to 2 inches for an average-sized shower. Framing below the mortar bed must be recessed by the maximum thickness of the mortar, if the finished floor surface is to align with the adjacent floor. Concrete slabs can simply be recessed by the required maximum mortar thickness. To support the heavy weight of the mortar and tile, the joists in a framed floor should be doubled or engineered for the load. After the subfloor has been installed, a 6-mil poly or felt cleavage membrane is applied over it to allow the wood structure to move without cracking the mortar and tiles. A waterproof shower pan consisting of 40-mil PVC plastic or copper goes on next, upon which the mortar bed is laid.

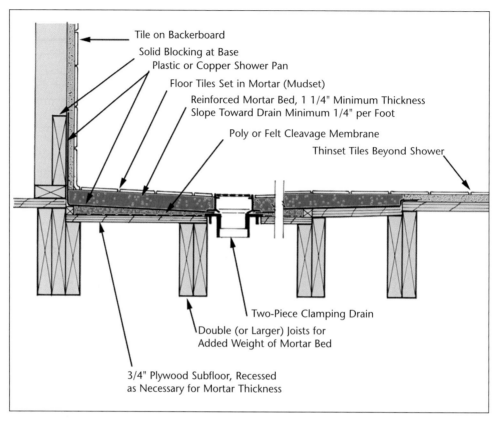

Tile on Backerboard
Solid Blocking at Base
Plastic or Copper Shower Pan
Floor Tiles Set in Mortar (Mudset)
Reinforced Mortar Bed, 1 1/4" Minimum Thickness
Slope Toward Drain Minimum 1/4" per Foot
Poly or Felt Cleavage Membrane
Thinset Tiles Beyond Shower
Two-Piece Clamping Drain
Double (or Larger) Joists for
Added Weight of Mortar Bed
3/4" Plywood Subfloor, Recessed
as Necessary for Mortar Thickness

Figure 12.4 Special detailing of a mudset shower floor is required to make it watertight. The floor is recessed to allow for the mortar bed and joists are doubled or upsized for the heavy masonry load. A cleavage membrane allows the wood to move without cracking the masonry. A cleavage membrane (or copper shower pan) keeps water out of the wood structure.

Resilient Flooring

Resilient flooring gets its name from the fact that it is flexible, unlike brittle mineral-based tiles. It comes in two forms, sheet goods and tiles, adhered to the substrate with troweled-on adhesive or adhesive pre-applied to the back of the tiles for a "peel-and-stick" installation directly to the substrate. Troweled-on adhesive is the more difficult, but more dependable installation method.

All resilient flooring requires an underlayment on framed floors (or plywood subflooring, if filled and sanded) but can install directly over a concrete slab that has been troweled smooth and filled. Resilient flooring can also be applied to existing flooring if it is tightly adhered, free of checks and voids and edge curls. If the existing floorcovering is dubious you will get a better job by having it removed, or, if possible, specifying a new plywood underlayment on top of it before the new floorcovering is applied. Resilient flooring should never be applied over concrete slabs subject to dampness or moisture, such as in many basements. If the slab isn't consistently dry, a subfloor on wood sleepers should be installed, before applying the flooring, as described in the following section.

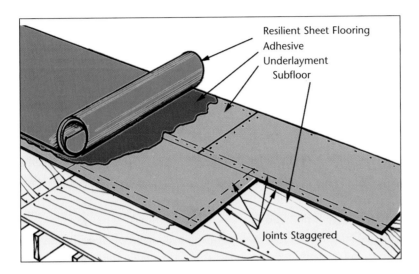

Resilient Sheet Flooring
Adhesive
Underlayment
Subfloor

Joints Staggered

Figure 12.5 Resilient flooring installs in troweled-on adhesive over a suitable underlayment. Note that the underlayment panels are installed so that the joints do not align with the joints in the subfloor.

Wood Flooring

The vulnerability of wood to moisture makes it a less practical option for baths than for kitchens, but that doesn't hamper its appeal to homeowners, so it nevertheless ends up in many baths. Two types are in use today:

- Glue-down strip/plank and parquet flooring

- Traditional strip or plank flooring

Glue-down strip and plank and parquet ("mosaic") flooring consist of hardwood veneer bonded to a thin plywood substrate. Both types install over underlayment or filled and sanded plywood subflooring, by means of troweled-on mastic. Glue-down wood flooring can be applied directly to concrete slabs if two conditions are met:

1. The slab is smooth and free of voids.

2. The slab is free of moisture.

Filling voids and grinding the slab smooth satisfies the first condition. The second is more of a challenge. Slabs in today's new homes are poured over a granular base with a vapor barrier, usually poly sheet. If you can ascertain your client's home was thus constructed, you can be relatively sure that the slab won't wick up moisture from the ground. Short of cutting through part of the slab, you won't likely be able to determine the construction of a slab in an existing home. You might find out by using an electronic moisture meter or employing a simple test. Tape a small piece of poly to the surface, and then check it after 24 hours. If condensation appears on the undersurface or the slab is damp, there is enough moisture to make installing a wood floor risky.

If the slab is such that a glue-down installation is iffy, there is another way to attach the flooring: specify a wood substrate anchored to the slab. The substrate can be either 3/4-inch (19 mm) plywood power-nailed to the slab or 2x4 wood sleepers, spaced 16 inches (406 mm) apart and power-nailed to the slab. In either case, a moisture barrier is required between the slab and wood substrate to keep moisture at bay.

Traditional wood flooring strips and planks consist of hardwood tongue-and-groove strips that require jobsite sanding and finishing or wood plank flooring that comes pre-finished. Both options are nominally 3/4 inch (19 mm) thick, in random lengths with tongue and groove edges on all four sides that interlock each piece to the next. Nails driven at angles through the tongue of each strip or plank holds it to the substrate. The interlock allows the pieces to shrink with changing moisture content, but not to move out of vertical alignment with each other.

Strips and planks can run in any direction over the floor to suit the design objectives, but for a squeak-free installation the flooring should run across the joists to allow nails to penetrate the joists. If the flooring runs in another direction, a solid subfloor with a minimum 3/4 inch (19 mm) thickness should underlie the flooring and the nails should penetrate the subfloor by at least 3/4 inch (19 mm).

Traditional wood strip flooring and plank flooring are installed over a concrete slab by means of sleepers, as described for glue-down flooring, except that the strips can be nailed directly to the sleepers without a subfloor.

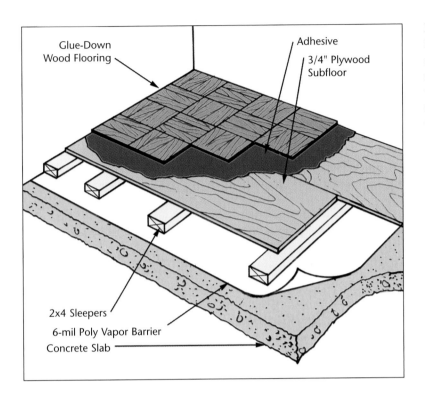

Figure 12.6 Glue-down wood flooring is applied to a plywood substrate with adhesive. If the floor is concrete, 2x4 sleepers support the plywood. A poly vapor barrier between the concrete and sleepers keeps moisture out of the wood above.

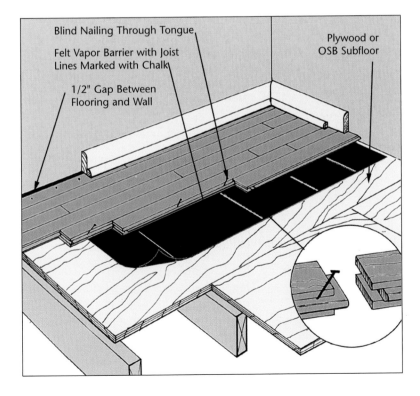

Figure 12.7 Wood-strip flooring is blind-nailed through the tongue of each strip (inset) through the subfloor and into the joists. The position of the joists can be determined from the nailing pattern on the subfloor, and then chalked onto the felt vapor barrier. The 1/2-inch gap at the walls allows the flooring to expand and contract.

181

Laminate Flooring

The newest floorcovering on the market is laminate. It consists of several layers of material bonded together under high pressure, similar to the laminate products used for countertops. A clear melamine top layer protects the design layer. Then follows a plastic resin-impregnated paper layer with wood grain pattern printed on. These are bonded to a structural fiberboard core, backed by a layer of melamine. The clear topmost wear layer is smooth and can be slippery when wet, making laminate flooring a questionable option for baths.

Installing laminate flooring entails applying glue to the tongue-and-groove edges of each piece and pressing it into the abutting piece on the floor, without actually attaching it to the floor. The finish floor then "floats" above the substrate. There are currently two choices of underlayments, a 1/4-inch (13 mm) thick, low-density fiber panel, 24 inch x 30 inch (610 mm x 762 mm), or closed-cell foam cushion, which is shipped in rolls. Laminate flooring installs over concrete slab floors in much the same way as over wood-framed floors, except that a poly vapor barrier is placed over the slab before the underlayment material.

Figure 12.8 Laminate strip flooring consists of a composite core overlaid with a pattern layer and a clear wear layer. Many patterns and colors are available. The strips are glued only on the edges and float on the floor over a foam plastic underlayment.

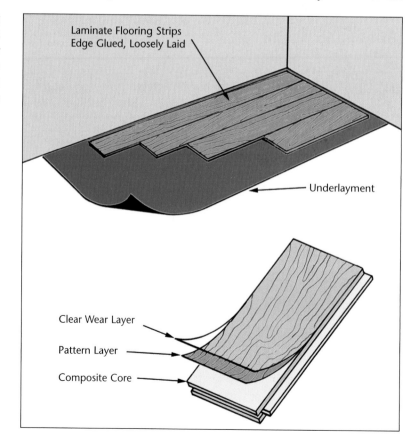

Laminate Flooring Strips
Edge Glued, Loosely Laid

Underlayment

Clear Wear Layer

Pattern Layer

Composite Core

WALL AND CEILING FINISH MATERIALS

Walls surrounding showers, baths and sinks are constantly subject to moisture, so a water-resistant finish that can be washed periodically is essential. Even bath walls outside the wettest areas are subject to the constant high levels of humidity and are prone to develop mold and fungus so they too should be washable. In the kitchen wall surfaces surrounding cooking areas are frequently spattered with grease and food scraps, so they too need to be able to withstand regular washings.

Paint

Paint is a versatile finish that can be quickly and easily applied to many substrates. With paint you can offer your client an unlimited variety of colors in several finishes. In time, your client can easily change the color by repainting. Though economical compared to other finishes, a quality paint job requires quality paint, a properly prepared substrate and competent application.

Paint is a liquid composed of a binder material, pigments and a solvent. The paints of the past contained lead and petroleum-based solvents. We now recognize that these ingredients are hazardous to health and have new formulas to compensate. For example, today's latex paints substitute non-toxic pigments for lead-based ones and water for petroleum-based solvents.

Paint suppliers use computer equipment to mix paints from their standard range or to any desired color. The **sheen** of a paint indicates its glossiness or flatness. There are five standard sheens:

- **Flat**. The dullest finish hides surface flaws but is hard to clean. Usually not considered washable so not recommended for bath walls or kitchen walls surrounding food preparation areas. Never a good choice for woodwork.

- **Eggshell**. Almost flat but with a slight bit of gloss making it a good choice for all but wet areas and those requiring frequent cleaning.

- **Satin**. Shinier still than flat but washable—a good choice for most walls and ceilings not requiring frequent cleaning.

- **Semi-Gloss**. A definite gloss, but somewhat dull. This sheen is washable, so a good choice for wet-area walls and ceilings and rooms where surfaces must be cleaned often, such as bathrooms, laundries, and kitchens. Also a good choice for woodwork in all rooms.

- **Gloss**. The shiniest sheen is the most washable finish. Gloss is the easiest to maintain in all but constantly wet areas, such as surrounding tubs and showers. Because of its high reflectivity, gloss is most likely to broadcast any flaws or unevenness in the substrate. For that reason, it is more often used on woodwork than wall surfaces.

Wallcoverings

Though many still call it "wallpaper," the product sold in rolls today probably contains paper only on the backside, if at all. The facing is vinyl, which is much more durable and easy to clean. Numerous colors and patterns are available, many with complimentary border strips.

The substrate should be perfectly smooth because any surface irregularities will telescope through a wallcovering. Vinyl wallcovering is a less than ideal surface material for walls surrounding baths and showers because of the potential for water getting behind the seams and causing the wallcovering to peel off.

Wood

Like paint, wood is a universal finish material available in many species and forms. It can be another item to add to your kitchen and bath design palette if you understand its limitations and installation requirements.

The first thing to recognize is that wood is an organic material that constantly changes in response to its environment. Heat and humidity cause it to swell. Cold and dryness cause it to shrink. Joints consequently open and close, inviting moisture to penetrate and grow mold and fungus. The pores in the surface of unfinished wood will also grow microorganisms in a moist environment.

It should come as no surprise that rough, unfinished barnwood would probably be the worst choice of a wall finish in a bath. Wood, in fact, should never be used around tubs and showers, with one exception: unfinished cedar or redwood inside saunas. If you specify wood on other kitchen and bath walls, make sure the surface is properly sealed. A gloss or semi-gloss enamel seals the surface and makes a good cleanable finish. If a natural finish is desired, the wood can be sealed with a penetrating oil or a natural surface finish such as varnish or polyurethane.

Wood is available in many species and shapes to suit many applications. We'll see some of the many ways wood is used for trim a bit further on. As a material for wall surfaces, the choices are veneer paneling, stile-and-rail paneling, board siding or plain boards. Veneer paneling consists of hardwood plywood installed directly over a substrate or over wood furring with edges butted or covered with a trim piece. Traditional stile-and-rail paneling is an assembly of solid panel boards of a wood such as oak, cherry, or walnut, whose edges are mortised and tenoned into a grillwork of muntins.

Figure 12.9 A wainscot using traditional paneling. Raised panels are set into stiles and rails and held in place by moldings around the edges.

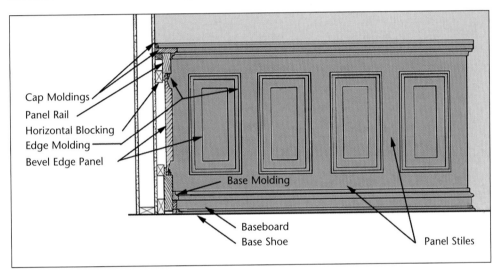

Cap Moldings
Panel Rail
Horizontal Blocking
Edge Molding
Bevel Edge Panel

Base Molding

Baseboard
Base Shoe

Panel Stiles

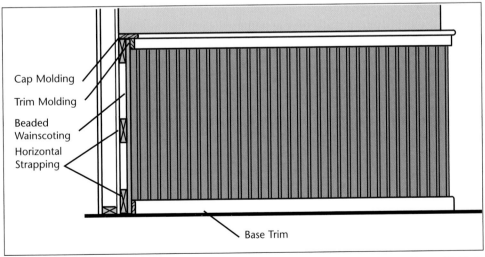

Cap Molding

Trim Molding

Beaded
Wainscoting

Horizontal
Strapping

Base Trim

Figure 12.10 A wainscot made up of tongue-and-groove board siding. If a vertical pattern is desired, the boards must be installed over horizontal furring strips.

The success of any wood wall surfacing depends as much on the visual characteristics of the wood as how it is put together. Dark colors darken a room. If that's what you want, you'll get a better job with a dark wood such as walnut, red oak, mahogany, cherry or redwood than with a light wood stained dark. If you don't want the wood color to darken the room but still want a natural finish, choose a lighter wood such as ash, birch, maple, white oak or pine. We'll talk more about natural wood finishes in the next chapter, in connection with wood trim. Obviously, you can paint the wood any color, but the wood should be a species that takes paint well, such as pine or poplar.

Laminate

Plastic laminate, or "laminate," can be applied to walls as well as countertops. One use is a continuous backsplash extending between a kitchen countertop and the wall cabinets. When used this way the laminate is applied with contact adhesive directly over wallboard.

Tile

Tile ranks as the number one material for wet areas so it's a natural for shower and tub surrounds and sink backsplashes. The many colors, shapes and sizes available today make tile an even more appealing part of your design palette.

Wall tile choices today extend beyond ceramic to include natural stone such as limestone, granite and marble. In helping your clients select wall tiles remember that tile is relatively permanent so encourage them to pick one they won't soon tire of. Select a color that anchors other colors in the room—fixtures, paint and wallcovering.

Tiles come in various sizes from 1 inch (25 mm) to up to around 10 inches (254 mm) square. Tiles larger than 4 inches (102 mm) usually come as single units, whereas those measuring 4 inches and smaller are usually attached to mesh backing panels 12 inches (305 mm) square for easier installation. Any shape and size can be applied to a wall. In dry areas wall tiles can be applied to any solid, dry substrate. Walls around tubs and showers should only go onto substrates not affected by water penetration, such as cement backerboards, as described at the beginning of this chapter. Most wall tile today is applied into a troweled-on Portland cement-based adhesive (thin-set application). After the adhesive sets cementitious grout is forced into the joints with a rubber trowel. Cleaning off the excess grout from the surface finishes the job.

CASE STUDY #6 –
TRANSFORMING A SMALL BATH

The best finishes can't make a poorly planned room function any better, but they can turn a merely functional room into a space that delights. Such was the case with a small bath in a California remodel.

Originally a closet that jutted into the space from an adjoining bedroom cramped the room. Moving the closet to another location helped open up the bath and created opportunities for re-thinking the floor plan. Relocating the toilet to the corner of the newly gained floor space improved the layout. The tub stayed in its end-wall location but was shifted and built into a surround with a seat at the shallow end to permit easier access. A pedestal sink, flanked by two wood cabinets, replaced the wall-hung lavatory.

With the function of the room improved, the designer focused on the finishing touches. The first step was to choose a beige color for the tub, toilet and lav, which became the anchor for other colors in the room. Large dark brown floor tiles provide contrast to the fixtures and the smaller light beige wall tiles applied to the tub surround and wainscot. The cherry finish on the two cabinets, horizontal trim piece above the tile, wainscot door and frame add warmth. The finishing touch is a mirror on the wall above the lav and side cabinets that extend from the wainscot to the ceiling. The mirror makes the room seem much larger than it actually is.

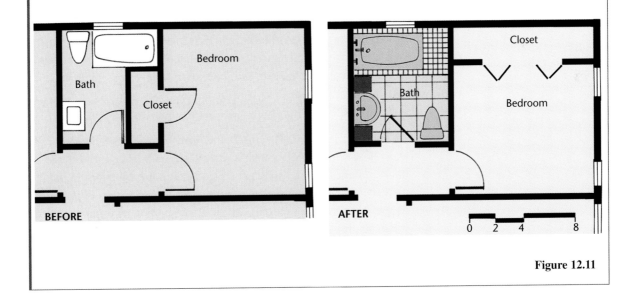

Figure 12.11

CHAPTER 13: Finishing Touches

In the previous chapter we scanned the materials that make up the surfaces of the floors, walls and ceilings of a room and the substrates under them. This final chapter will cover the small details necessary to complete the finish work of the interior.

TRIMMING THE INTERIOR

Unless they abut each other, as a tile wall does where it meets a tile floor, some kind of transitional element is needed between every intersecting surface in a room. This element is usually a linear piece of trimwork with a profile that suits its application and design intent

Contemporary homes use trimwork sparingly and employ simple shapes as baseboards and casings around doors and windows. More elaborate trimwork adorns the interiors of older homes. These might include a crown mold cornice around the edges of the ceilings, a horizontal band (picture rail) a few feet down on the walls and another band (chair rail) about waist height above the floor, to separate the flat wall above from the wainscot below. Matching this kind of elaborate woodwork can be difficult and expensive today. You might have to compromise by using less trim or simpler trim skillfully chosen to blend with the existing trimwork without slavishly copying it.

The trim in a room begins at the joint between the floor and the wall. Base trim usually consists of two pieces attached to the wall: a flat **baseboard** and a smaller toe piece called a **base shoe**. In quality work, base trim is always mitered at the corner joints. If joints are required for straight sections, the pieces are joined by joints "scarfed" on an angle, rather than simply butted together. **Casings** make the transition between door and window frames and their adjoining walls. They can be as simple as a single flat 1x4 or stock casing that runs around three sides of the window or door or as complex as an assembly of fluted moldings and rosettes. Windows may also require **stools** at the base and **aprons** between the stool and the wall.

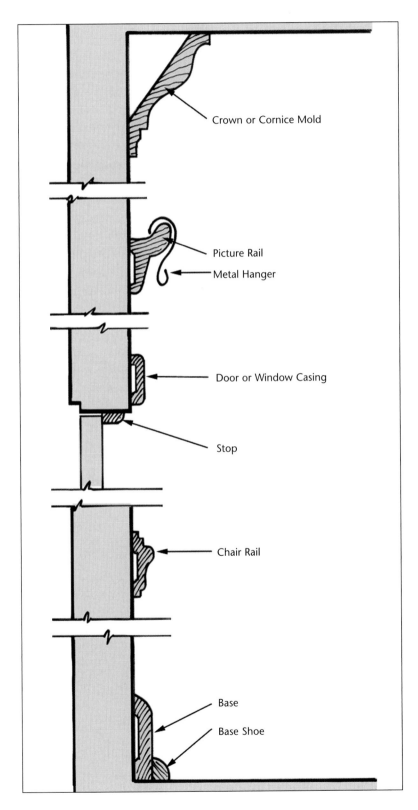

Figure 13.1 Moldings serve many purposes on interior walls, making transitions between surfaces and features such as windows, doors and wainscoting. For example, a chair rail can demarcate the wallcovering of a wainscot from a painted wall surface above.

Crown or Cornice Mold

Picture Rail

Metal Hanger

Door or Window Casing

Stop

Chair Rail

Base

Base Shoe

Wood Moldings

While some trim is a special shape or color of the same material used on the surface—such as the base and cap pieces used to terminate ceramic tile or the vinyl base that might edge resilient floorcoverings—wood reigns as the most universal trim material. Lumberyards usually stock scores of different trim profiles pre-milled out of ponderosa pine and can order many of the same shapes in oak, cherry, mahogany and walnut. Hardwood trim takes a variety of natural finishes, stained or unstained. Softwoods can also be naturally finished, but each has limitations. Pine absorbs penetrating stain unevenly, resulting in a splotchy appearance. All light-colored softwoods tend to yellow over time, a drawback if a lasting light color is desired. The random lengths that make up pre-milled pine casings are often of slightly different color, which is apparent at the finger joint splices. The color difference easily shows through any light-colored natural finish. This can be overcome by applying a non-penetrating stain prior to the final transparent finish.

Figure 13.2 Wood moldings come in many profiles. Pine is commonly stocked, but other species are available on order.

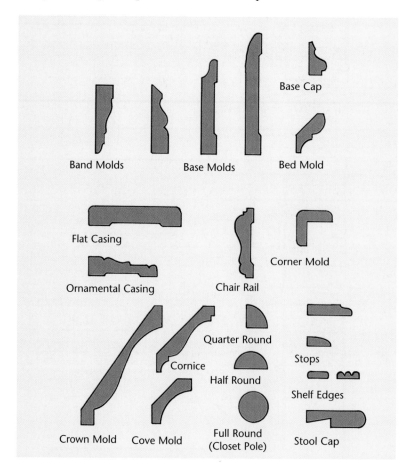

Band Molds · Base Molds · Bed Mold · Base Cap · Flat Casing · Ornamental Casing · Chair Rail · Corner Mold · Cornice · Quarter Round · Half Round · Crown Mold · Cove Mold · Full Round (Closet Pole) · Stops · Shelf Edges · Stool Cap

Manufactured Moldings

In a traditional remodel you may be faced with matching existing ornate wood or plaster trimwork. You might do this by joining several stock wood moldings into composite assemblies, though this requires a high level of craftsmanship and can be costly. Instead consider selecting from the variety of classical molding shapes now manufactured from such materials as polyurethane or fiberglass-reinforced polyester. Unlike wood, manufactured moldings aren't affected by changes in humidity. Cornices, columns, friezes, niches and medallions are some of the many shapes available. These moldings are typically pre-primed and either nailed or applied with adhesive from a caulking gun. After installation, they can be painted with latex or oil paints. An increasingly large variety of products are available from specialty manufacturers as well as cabinet manufacturers, who often offer moldings as accessories.

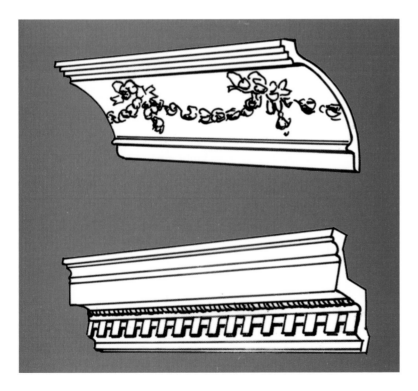

Figure 13.3 Moldings with complex surface designs, such as these cornice molds, are made from various plastic and cementitious materials that, unlike wood, don't shrink and crack.

NATURAL WOOD FINISHES

One of the reasons you might select a particular species of wood for an interior application, such as a door, casing, or trim, is its appearance. A natural finish is the only way to let its unique color, texture and grain show through. Even so, you might want to temper the expression of these features by varying the sheen, depth and color of the finish. A wide range of natural finishes with different levels of opacity, color and surface durability stand ready to help you obtain the desired end result. To make the correct choice you must understand the functional requirements of the application, the nature of the wood species, the color and sheen sought by the customer and finally, the products available to suit the job.

As with paints, formulations for natural finishes have constantly evolved over the years. Some oil- and lacquer-based coatings now have non-toxic water-based (waterborne) alternatives. However, the newer products don't always yield the same appearance as the formulations they replaced and require different application techniques. Clear latex floor finish, for example, is harder to apply and looks milkier than polyurethane, which is oil based.

All natural finishes are either **penetrating** or **film-forming** finishes, depending on whether they seep down into the matrix of the wood or build a film on the surface. Penetrating finishes bring out all of the nuances of the grain and color of the wood, resulting in a rich "bare wood" appearance. Not all woods have the qualities that show up best with penetrating finishes though. Hardwoods tend to take them much better than softwoods. Pine, for example, sucks in a penetrating finish unevenly, resulting in spottiness. Even among hardwoods, species with a lot of character such as walnut or teak fare better than those with more subtle grain or nondescript character, such as birch or maple.

Penetrating Finishes

Penetrating finishes include three basic formulations, oil, resin and varnish, all of which are solvent based. **Boiled linseed oil** is the most traditional oil finish. It requires several coats and dries slowly, yielding a warm (yellowish), slightly dull patina. **Tung oil** is a natural oil finish highly resistant to abrasion, moisture, heat, acid and mildew. **Mineral oil** is similar and can be used safely on food preparation surfaces, such as butcher blocks. When specifying a penetrating oil finish for butcher blocks used for food preparation, include language that guarantees the product is safe for culinary surfaces. **Penetrating resins and stains** are polymer-based finishes that bring out the best of hard, open-grain woods such as oak. Danish oil and antique oil are varieties of this material. Penetrating stains on pine and certain other softwoods result in an uneven color, since the wood absorbs the colorant in the stain at different degrees. This can be overcome by first priming the wood with a pre-stain wood conditioner. **Rub-on varnish** combines penetrating resins with varnish to build up a higher sheen than oils or resins.

Film-Forming Finishes

Surface finishes include solvent, lacquer and water-based products. **Shellac** yields a dull sheen but can be rubbed to a higher sheen. White shellac yellows the wood slightly; orange shellac much more so. Shellac thins with alcohol and dries quickly. It makes a good sealer for other finishes but does not resist heat and moisture or alcohol well when used alone. **Lacquer** can also be rubbed to a high gloss, forming a strong, clear finish but one vulnerable to moisture. Because it dries too fast to brush on easily, it is usually sprayed on in several thin coats, making it a better factory than site-applied finish. Lacquer thins with lacquer thinner, which is harmful to breathe or touch. **Spar varnish** and **polyurethane varnish** are two solvent-based clear finishes that stand up very well to water, heat and alcohol. That's why spar varnish has long been the finish of choice for ship decks. Both are thinned with mineral spirits (paint thinner) and are brushed on. Polyurethane is an excellent finish for wood floors, available in satin or gloss sheen.

All water-based finishes are of the film-forming type. They yield stable color and do not yellow when used over light-colored woods—an important plus to today's preference for blond-colored floors. On the other hand, the appearance is not the same as with solvent-based finishes. You should compare actual samples before specifying one option over the other. Also, raised grain has plagued waterborne finishes since their market debut. While products continue to improve, they must still be applied in strict accordance with the manufacturer's recommendations for success. The best waterborne finishes ship in two containers. The finish, itself, is in one, a catalyst in the other. When mixed together the catalyst causes the finish to cure.

Colorants

When the natural color of the wood won't do, or when you want to compensate for the yellowing effect many wood finishes produce, apply a stain before the finish coating, whether the finish is penetrating or film forming.

There are two basic types of wood stains. **Pigmented stains** contain finely ground colorants suspended in oil or solvent, much the same as a thin, opaque paint. This type of stain coats the wood, similar to a surface finish. It works best over light woods with nondescript grain character. **Dyed stains** contain organic derivatives dissolved, rather than suspended, in the medium. They penetrate into the grain, allowing it to show through. Both types are available in oil- or water-based solvents.

A

ACQ: Ammonia copper quaternary, an emerging chemical treatment alternative to chromated copper arsenic (CCA), used to preserve wood from attack by insects and fungus.

Apron: A horizontal casing below a window stool (interior).

B

Backerboard: A panel material used as a substrate for tile on floors and wall surfaces in wet areas.

Band Joist: The floor joist that runs around the perimeter of the house above the foundation.

Beam: A horizontal or nearly horizontal framing member that supports loads imposed perpendicular to the long axis introduced by other framing such as joists.

Beeswax: A wood preservative considered non-toxic.

Blueboard: A type of gypsum wallboard (drywall) with a blue-colored, paper facing chemically treated to provide a bonding surface for plaster or tile adhesive.

Borax: A wood preservative considered non-toxic.

C

CCA: Chromated copper arsenic; a chemical used in pressure-treated lumber.

Cement Backerboard: (see "Backerboard").

Chord: An outer member of a truss (top chord, bottom chord).

Chair Rail: A trim piece that runs horizontally on a wall at the height of a chair back. Used to make the transition between a wainscot and upper wall.

Cleavage Membrane: A thin, waterproof material such as polyethylene or asphalt-saturated felt, placed between a rigid finish material, such as floor tile and a

substrate, such as a wood floor, to allow the substrate to move without cracking the finish material.

Collar Tie: A horizontal framing member installed between opposite sloping rafters to counter the outward thrust of the roof.

Column: A vertical framing member that supports loads parallel to its long axis.

Conduction: The flow of heat energy through a material. Heat flows from the warmer to cooler side of the material.

Convection: The transmission of heat through a liquid or gas. The cooler feeling you experience in front of a fan in summer is due to convective air movement over your skin.

Crawl Space: An open space between the first floor and ground, usually high enough to crawl through.

D

Daylighting: Using light from the sun to light the interior of a building.

Dead Load: A force on the building that is constant, resulting from the weight of the building materials and built-in items that are not likely to change, such as a spa.

Deflection: The maximum vertical distance by which horizontal framing members sag.

Divided Light: A type of window or door containing several sections of glazing, each section, or pane, separated from the other by muntins. If muntins go all the way through the glazing, the assembly is called true divided light. If the muntins are applied to the face of the glazing, the assembly is called simulated divided light.

Dormer: A structure built atop a roof to increase the usable space below or to contain windows.

Drywall: Gypsum-based plaster encased between two layers of facing paper, used for interior wall surfaces as a substrate for paint, wallpaper or tile finishes.

E

EER: Energy Efficiency Rating, a standard for rating the energy efficiency of an appliance. The higher the EER number, the more efficient the appliance.

EIF: A composite Exterior Insulation and Finish exterior wall cladding, consisting of a layer of rigid foam over which is applied a stucco-like finish made of a polymeric matrix and stone dust. Sometimes EIF coatings are applied directly to the sheathing if other provisions for insulation are made.

Engineered Lumber: Structural members composed of wood fibers bonded by resins and formed into structurally efficient post, beam and joist shapes.

Envelope: The outermost parts of a building that separate the interior environment from the outside weather, usually the walls and roof.

EPDM: Ethylene propylene diene monomer, a synthetic membrane material used for roofing flat or nearly flat surfaces.

Expanded Metal Lath: A type of mesh used as a backing for plaster or mortar.

F

Face Framing: A method of installing joists or rafters, where they attach to the face of the beam rather than run over the top.

Felt: Asphalt-saturated felt (or building paper, tar paper) used as a weatherproof underlayment for roofing and siding materials.

Footing: A pad that distributes the weight of the structure on the earth.

Foundation: The below-grade portion of the structure between the footing and main level.

Furring: Thin strips installed on a wall or ceiling surface to create a substrate for a finish material (also called "strapping").

G

Girder: A horizontal framing member that supports beams. The terms girder and beam are often used interchangeably.

Glazing: The transparent material in a window or door.

Grade Beam: A type of shallow foundation consisting of a reinforced concrete rim, most used with slab-on-grade floors without basements in regions without seasonal frosts.

Gyp-Board: (see "drywall").

Gypsum Backerboard: (see "Backerboard").

Gypsum Drywall: (see "drywall").

Gypsum Wallboard: (see "drywall").

H

Hand: A term that describes a door by the way it opens. The hand is the side of the door on which the hinges are mounted when you are standing outside the door.

Head: The portion of the door or window assembly at the top, including the fixed and movable parts of the window or door and the fixed portion of the building into which the window or door mounts.

Header: A beam above a window or door opening.

HVAC: Heating Ventilating and Air Conditioning.

I

I-Joist: A manufactured wood or wood composition joist consisting of a thin plywood or OSB web encased between solid wood or plywood flanges.

J

Jamb: The portion of the door or window assembly at the sides, including the fixed and movable parts of the window or door and the fixed portion of the building into which the window or door mounts.

Joist: A level or nearly level member used in series to frame a floor or ceiling structure.

K

Knot: A portion of a branch or limb that extends into the trunk of a tree and appears as a darker spot on sawn lumber.

L

Laminated Veneer Lumber: (see "LVL").

Ledger, Ledger Board: A board attached to a wall as a support for joists.

Life Cycle Cost: The total cost of a material or device, including its initial cost plus the cost of operation over its expected lifetime.

Light: As applied to windows, a light is a single section of glass.

Lindane: A chemical wood preservative considered toxic.

Linseed Oil: A wood preservative considered non-toxic.

Live Load: A force on the building structure that acts intermittently, such as wind, snow, earthquakes, or the weight of people and their equipment.

LVL: Abbreviation for "laminated veneer lumber," a manufactured material composed of thin layers of lumber veneer pressure-bonded together with grain running in the same direction, used for joists and beams.

M

Miter: An angular joint between two intersecting pieces.

Molding: A strip of material cut, shaped or embossed to make the transition between two dissimilar surfaces.

Mortise: A rectangular recess cut in the edge of one piece to receive another piece, such as a tenon, or a door lockset.

Mudsetting: A method of installing ceramic stone tiles by setting them into a mortar bed.

Muntin: A small vertical or horizontal strip that divides windowpanes from each other.

N

Nailer: A piece of material attached to the main structure as a base for attaching subsequent items.

O

Oriented Strand board (OSB): A panel product made by bonding wood chips together with a resin under high heat and pressure. OSB panels are used mainly for roof and wall sheathing.

Outgassing: The slow release of chemical gasses contained within building materials to the ambient air, such as formaldehyde in particleboard.

Overflow Scupper: A projecting lip at the edge of a flat roof, which allows water to run off the edge.

P

Parallel Strand Lumber, PSL: Structural framing shapes made from wood fibers that run parallel to the long axis of the member.

Particle Board: A panel product made from sawdust or wood particles, bonded with a resin under high heat and pressure.

Pentachlorophenol: A chemical wood preservative considered toxic.

Picture Rail: A horizontal trim piece installed high up on a wall as a means of hanging pictures without puncturing the wall with nails or brads.

Plywood: A panel product made by cross-laminating alternate thin layers of wood.

Poly, Polyethylene: A type of plastic with many uses in construction, one of which is for vapor barriers in walls, ceilings, roofs and under slabs.

Potash: A wood preservative considered non-toxic.

R

Rabbet: An L-shaped recess cut out of the edge of a board or panel, usually to allow an adjacent piece to overlap it in the same plane.

Radiation: The emission of energy from an object. Heat waves from the object radiate to cooler objects. Like radio waves, this form of energy passes through air without heating it, only becoming heat after it strikes and is absorbed by a dense material.

Rafters: Structural members used in series to support roofs.

Rail: One of the horizontal structural parts of a door panel.

Ridge Beam: A beam placed at the peak or ridge of a gable roof to support the high end of the rafters.

Ridge Board: A board into which rafters terminate at a roof ridge and which serves as a nailer for the roof sheathing at the ridge.

R-Value: A measure of resistance to the passage of heat through a material by conductance, in British Thermal Units per Hour (BTUH). Used to rate the heat resisting ability of building insulation. The higher the R-value, the more effective the insulation.

S

Scarf Joint: A joint between two straight pieces of trim or woodwork where each piece meets the other one on an angle other than 90 degrees (butt joint), such that any shrinkage will be less noticeable.

Scupper: (see "Overflow Scupper").

SEER: Seasonal Energy Efficiency Rating: energy efficiency rating (SEER). A standard for rating the annual energy efficiency of appliances, based on the effects of climate. The higher the EER, the more efficient the appliance.

Shear: The horizontal force that impels two items in contact to slide past each other.

Sheathing: A material such as plywood used to cover studs or joists, tying them together into a single structural system and providing a base for attaching finish materials.

Sheen: The surface glossiness, or luster, of paints, ranging from "flat," the dullest, to "gloss," the shiniest.

Sill: The portion of the door or window assembly at the bottom or floor, including the fixed and movable parts of the window or door and the fixed portion of the building into which the window or door mounts.

SIP: Structural insulated panel; a composite wall or roof cladding system consisting of a rigid foam insulation sandwiched between an inner and outer sheet of nailbase sheathing, usually plywood or oriented strand board.

Sister: An auxiliary stud or joist attached to the primary member to add strength or even out the surface.

Skim-Coat Plaster: A plaster process where a thin layer of plaster is troweled onto a special type of gypsum wallboard called blueboard.

Slump: The vertical distance wet concrete sags in a test cone, when the cone is pulled up off the concrete.

Soda: A wood preservative considered non-toxic.

Soffit: A lowered portion of a ceiling. The horizontal surface below the eave. A porch roof.

Solid Surfacing: A class of rigid surfacing materials made of acrylic and/or polyester resins mixed with alumina tryhydrate.

Stem wall foundation: A foundation extending down to the frost line used to enclose a crawl space in place of a full basement.

Stile: One of the vertical structural parts of the door panel in a stile-and-rail door.

Strapping: (see "Furring").

T

Thermal Break: An insulating gasket placed between the inside and outside portions of a metal window or door frame to stem heat loss and minimize condensation.

Thinset, Thinsetting: A method for installing cementitious, ceramic and stone tiles on a substrate, by setting the tiles into a special mortar compound troweled onto the substrate.

Thrust: The outward force that a sloping roof imposes on the walls.

To Weather: The vertical dimension of the exposed face of siding or shingles.

Transom: A horizontal window set above a door or other windows.

Trim: (see "Molding").

Tributyl Tin Oxide (TBTO): A chemical wood preservative considered toxic.

U

Underlayment: A non-structural sheet material installed on a subfloor to provide a stable, level and smooth base for the floorcovering.

Ultraviolet: An invisible portion of the light spectrum that fades fabrics.

V

Veneer: A thin sheet of material bonded to one or more other materials. Plywood is one example of a veneer material.

W

Wainscot: A material used to clad the lower portion of a wall.

Wallboard: (see "Drywall").

Web: The interior members of a truss or thin center portion of a beam or I-joist.

RESOURCES

CODE DEVELOPER ASSOCIATIONS

International Association of Plumbing & Mechanical Officials (IAPMO)
5001 E. Philadelphia Street
Ontario, CA 91761
Phone 909-472-4100 • iapmo.org

International Code Council, Inc. (ICC)
5203 Leesburg Pike, Suite 600,
Falls Church, VA 22041-3401
Phone 703-931-4533 • iccsafe.org

National Fire Protection Association (NFPA)
Batterymarch Park, P.O. Box 9101,
Quincy, MA 02269-9101
Phone 617-770-3000 • nfpa.org

National Research Council of Canada
1200 Montreal Road, Building M-58, Ottawa,
Ontario, Canada K1A
Phone 613-993-9101 • nrc.ca

TRADE ASSOCIATIONS

American National Standards Institute (ANSI)
1430 Broadway, New York, NY 10018
Phone 212-642-4980 • ansi.org

American Society for Testing and Materials (ASTM)
100 Barr Harbor Drive,
West Conshohocken, PA 19428-2959
Phone 610-832-9585 • astm.org

The Association of Pool & Spa Professionals (APSP)
2111 Eisenhower Avenue, Alexandria, VA 22314
Phone 703-838-0083 • theapsp.org

National Association of Home Builders (NAHB)
1201 15th Street, NW, Washington, DC 20005
Phone 800-368-5242 • nahb.org

National Association of the Remodeling Industry (NARI)
1901 No. Moore St., Suite 808, Arlington, VA 22209
Phone 800-611-6274 • nari.org

National Electrical Manufacturing Association (NEMA)
780 Lee Street, Suite 200, Des Plaines, IL 60016
Phone 800-611-6274 • nema.org

National Kitchen & Bath Association (NKBA)
687 Willow Grove Street, Hackettstown, NJ 07840
Phone 908-852-0033 • nkba.org

Sheet Metal and Air Conditioning Contractors' National Association (SMACNA)
4201 Lafayette Center Drive,
Chantilly, VA 21151-1209
Phone 703-803-2980 • smacna.org

Underwriters Laboratories, Inc. (UL)
333 Pfingsten Road,
Northbrook, IL 60062-2096
Phone 847-272-8800 • ul.com

GAMA – An Association of Appliance & Equipment Manufacturers
2107 Wilson Blvd., Suite 600, Arlington, VA 22201
Phone 703-525-7060 • gamanet.org